APPALACHIAN TRAIL

Data Book

2 0 1 7

APPALACHIAN TRAIL

Data Book

2017

THIRTY-NINTH EDITION

Daniel D. Chazin, *Editor*

APPALACHIAN TRAIL
CONSERVANCY®

Harpers Ferry

Contents

Notice to All Trail Users

The information in this publication is the result of the best effort of the publisher, using data available to it at the time of printing. Changes resulting from maintenance work and relocations are constantly occurring and, therefore, no published route can be regarded as precisely accurate at the time you read this notice.

Notices of pending relocations are indicated in current Appalachian Trail guidebooks, whenever possible.

Because maintenance of the Trail is conducted by volunteers and maintaining clubs listed in the appropriate guidebooks, questions about the exact route of the Trail should be addressed to the maintaining clubs or the Appalachian Trail Conservancy, P.O. Box 807, Harpers Ferry, WV 25425 (telephone: 304-535-6331; e-mail: <info@appalachiantrail.org>). On the Trail, please pay close attention to — and follow — the white blazes and any directional signs.

There are few things more rewarding than hiking the Appalachian Trail, whether you come to it as a novice looking to spend only a couple of hours outdoors or a Trail-tested veteran who has thru-hiked more than once.

Regardless of your skill, it is extremely important to plan your hike, especially in places where water is scarce. Purify water drawn from any source. Water purity cannot be guaranteed. The Appalachian Trail Conservancy and the various maintaining clubs attempt to locate good sources of water along the Trail but have no control over those sources and cannot, in any sense, be responsible for the quality of the water at any given time. You should ensure the safety of all water you use by treating it.

Certain risks are inherent in any Appalachian Trail hike. Each A.T. user must accept personal responsibility for his or her safety while on the Trail. The Appalachian Trail Conservancy and its member maintaining clubs cannot ensure the safety of any hiker on the Trail, and, when undertaking a hike on the Trail, each user thereby assumes the risk for any accident, illness, or injury that might occur on the Trail.

Enjoy your hike, but please take all appropriate precautions for your safety and well-being.

Safety and Ethics

Although the Appalachian Trail is safer than most places, you should be aware that problems do occur, and a few crimes of violence have occurred during the past three decades. Safety awareness is one of your best lines of defense. Be aware of what you are doing, where you are, and to whom you are talking. Here are some suggestions:

- *Use extra caution if hiking alone.* If you are by yourself and encounter a stranger who makes you feel uncomfortable, say you are with a group that is behind you. Be creative. If in doubt, move on.

- *Leave your hiking itinerary and timetable* with someone at home. Be sure he or she knows your Trail name, if you have one. Check in regularly, and establish a procedure to follow if you fail to check in. It helps to let ATC know your name and Trail name, in case a family member needs to reach you during an extended hike. However, *do not broadcast your itinerary or location in real time* on on-line journals or blogs.

- *Be wary of strangers.* Be friendly, but cautious. Don't tell strangers your plans. Avoid people who act suspiciously, hostile, or intoxicated.

- *Don't camp near road crossings.*

- *Carrying firearms is strongly discouraged.* Although it is now legal to carry (but not discharge) on National Park Service lands and in most other areas, with the proper state-by-state permits, they could be turned against you, you face a high risk of an accidental shooting, and they are extra weight.

- *Eliminate opportunities for theft.* Don't bring jewelry. Hide your money. If you must leave your pack, hide it carefully, or leave it with someone trustworthy. Don't leave valuables or equipment (especially in sight) in vehicles parked at Trailheads.

- *Use the Trail and shelter registers.* Sign in, leave a note, and report any suspicious activities. If someone needs to locate you, or if a serious crime has been committed along the Trail, the first place authorities will look is in the registers.

- *Report any crime or harassment* to the local law-enforcement authorities *and* then ATC. Send an e-mail to <incident@appalachiantrail.org> or call (304) 535-6331.

As the A.T. becomes increasingly used, the potential for problems could increase. Help to keep the Trail a safe place. Maintain your safety awareness, help each other, and report all incidents. *More detailed advice is available at <www.appalachiantrail.org/safetyawareness>.* Be prudent and cautious without allowing common sense to slip into paranoia. Trust your gut.

Reporting Trail Emergencies

Check the map, guidebook, nearest shelter, or Trailhead facility for local emergency telephone numbers. Leave the Trail at the nearest road crossing, and find a telephone or cellular-phone reception. Know your location and the location of the incident as precisely as possible. Dial "911" or "0" (ask the operator to connect you with the nearest state-police facility), and make your report. Ask the officer to notify the Appalachian Trail Conservancy at (304) 535-6331.

Public Transportation and Shuttles

The Appalachian Trail Conservancy maintains information on public transportation to the Trail and available shuttle providers on its Web site at <www.appalachiantrail.org/home/explore-the-trail/transportation-options>.

Leave No Trace™

The Appalachian Trail Conservancy, in partnership with the Leave No Trace Center for Outdoor Ethics, asks you to help take care of the Appalachian Trail and the wild country it passes through. Please do your part by following the seven Leave No Trace principles of low-impact use while in the backcountry:

1. Plan ahead and prepare.
2. Travel and camp on durable surfaces.
3. Dispose of waste properly.
4. Leave what you find.
5. Minimize campfire impacts.
6. Respect wildlife.
7. Be considerate of other visitors.

More specific ways those principles apply to the Appalachian Trail can be found at <www.appalachiantrail.org/Lnt>. The continued existence of the Trail depends, in part, on proper use by those who walk on it. Particular care should be taken not to damage the footpath itself, natural features alongside it, or the property of others, through littering or other vandalism, improper fires, or use of vehicles. The needs of other users should always be considered, and special regulations must be followed in many areas. Please keep day-hiking groups to 25 people or fewer and overnight groups to no more than 10 people.

Although more than 99 percent of the Appalachian Trail now crosses public land, the remainder is on private or municipal property, thanks to the cooperation and good faith of the landowners. The Conservancy and its member clubs strongly urge all users of the Trail to respect those private lands and the owners' rights as if the lands were their own.

Public lands are, in a sense, the user's own—shared with all other users—so please proceed accordingly, taking care to obey any regulations imposed on use of the Trail in a particular section. **For example, camping permits are required before entering Great Smoky Mountains National Park.** On many other parts of the Trail, camping is permitted only in designated areas.

Again, please consult the guidebooks and maps, and watch for special signs along the Trail.

And, enjoy your hike!

Useful Features of the *A.T. Data Book*

This publication provides a ready reference for hikers to the major features of the Appalachian Trail as it winds for almost 2,190 miles from Maine to Georgia. Many hikers find it indispensable to their journeys on the A.T. and save each year's edition with a record of their experiences and accomplishments.

The features listed here include shelters and campsites, road crossings, sources of water, elevations, principal mountain peaks and gaps, and other notable physical landmarks of America's foremost national scenic trail. Locations of areas where lodging, meals, groceries, and post offices are available also are listed, with distances and directions. Additionally, each section is marked with the Trail-maintaining club associated with that segment, and Web-site information for the clubs may be found on page 85.

The *Data Book* is intended to be useful in broad-scale planning of a trip of any length on the Trail, from home or while on the footpath itself.

The *Data Book* does not, however, include sufficient detail for careful, complete planning of a trip. Potential hikers are encouraged to purchase separately the official *Appalachian Trail Guide* book-and-maps set for the state(s) they plan to hike (not to be confused with the *A.T. Guide* thru-hiking book from a commercial publisher). The guidebooks contain detailed descriptions of Trail sections, facilities near the Trail, points of interest off the Trail, background on the history and natural features of the area, and other important information.

All guidebooks are sold with sets of maps for the state(s) described, another key to a safe and enjoyable hike. Guidebooks, maps, and other ATC publications may be ordered by visiting the Ultimate A.T. Store *via* <www.atctrailstore.org>. Or, call (304) 728-5143 or toll-free to (888) 287-8673 (AT STORE). Membership in the Appalachian Trail Conservancy carries with it a discount on guidebooks and other publications.

The compilation of each edition of the *Data Book* begins with the latest *Appalachian Trail Guides*. The distances and descriptive information are updated to take into account relocations since the last edition.

This information is supplied to the Conservancy by its member clubs and volunteers who help ensure access to the Appalachian Trail experience for all. Each year, more than 6,000 volunteers contribute more than 200,000 hours of work to various projects along the Trail.

The data has been cross-checked by both volunteers and staff members. However, it is impossible to ensure absolute accuracy of the information, and changes may occur during the year of this edition. Trail-enhancing relocations that affect distances between major features are underway in some states. Also, severe weather conditions, fires, and other unpredictable developments might force temporary closings of a section.

Users of the Trail for any period of time should carefully follow the painted white blazes and signs that mark the current route of the Trail.

Hikers finding errors or omissions in the *Data Book* are urged to report them, by e-mail to <publisher@appalachiantrail.org>, or by mail to Data Book Editor, Appalachian Trail Conservancy, P.O. Box 807, Harpers Ferry, WV 25425. Confirmed changes will be included in the next edition.

How to Use the *Data Book*

The *Data Book* is divided into twelve chapters, beginning with Maine (at Katahdin) and ending with the Approach Trail to Springer Mountain in Georgia. With one exception, each chapter corresponds to a volume in the current series of *Appalachian Trail Guides* (see page 4 for ordering information). The section beginning on page 27, for example, matches the third volume in the guidebook series, which covers the Trail in Massachusetts–Connecticut. The exception is the Trail route through the Great Smokies of Tennessee and North Carolina, which is covered in both the Tennessee–North Carolina and North Carolina–Georgia guidebooks. It is included here only in Chapter Ten (Tennessee–North Carolina).

Trail-maintaining clubs are listed in the outside margins next to the section(s) of Trail that each club maintains. The beginning and ending points of each club's range are indicated by a small gray rectangle. Web site information for the clubs may be found on page 85.

Georgia A.T. Club

Trail sections, as numbered and identified in the corresponding guide, are given in the columns to the left on each page, under the heading *GBS* (guidebook section). Sections are numbered consecutively, from north to south, within each state.

N.C. Section 11

In the right column, under the heading *Map*, the number of the map that covers the area is given. For more detail about a particular feature or section of the Trail, consult the relevant guidebook section or map.

Each section contains a list of features along or near the Trail.

Towns with post offices (P.O.) are printed in boldface and carry their ZIP Code in the listing. Towns without post offices are listed only if the Trail goes directly through them; "P.O." is omitted in those cases.

Greenwood Lake, N.Y., P.O. 10925

The *elevations* of selected points along the Trail follow the name of the feature. Those elevations are intended to represent the most significant points in terms of elevation gain and loss and provide the hiker with a general sense of the elevation change along each section of the hike. Of course, many ups and downs have not been referenced in this book, and the difficulty of the terrain may vary considerably. Hikers should use the elevations provided only as a general guide.

Rainbow Ledges (1,517')

In general, all *facilities* within five miles of the Trail by road are included, unless similar facilities are located closer to the footpath or a facility's inclusion would not significantly benefit the hiker. In some cases, where a particular facility is not available for a great distance, we have included facilities that are more than five miles from the Trail but still within 12 miles.

To the right of the list of features, facilities, if any, are noted with a one-letter code. The codes are explained on pages 8–9.

Low Gap   Cw

Except for shelters, campsites, and water sources located on the Trail it-self—or within 0.1 mile of the footpath—the listing for a facility includes the distance and direction to it. So, if the symbols "C", "S", or "w" appear without direction and distance information in the listing, that campsite, shelter, or water source is on the Trail or within about 500 feet of it.

The number to the left of a feature is the *distance* — in miles — of the feature from the northern end of the part of the Trail covered in that particular chapter (read down). The number to the right of the features and facilities lists, correspondingly, is the feature's distance from the southern end of the part of the Trail covered by this chapter (read up). The starting point for the cumulative distance is given at the top of the column.

Miles from Katahdin		*Miles from Maine–N.H. Line*
0.0	Katahdin (Baxter Peak) (5,268')	281.8
1.0	Thoreau Spring	w 280.8

Sometimes the Trail follows a road, ridge line, lake, creek, or other physical feature for some distance. In those cases, usually only one distance is listed. For roads, this is generally the point at which the Trail first reaches the road proceeding from north to south, or, in some cases, the point representing the end of the section. For ridge lines, this is the highest point. Again, for more complete information about a particular feature, please consult the guide-books, maps, or both.

Codes

C   *Campsites and campgrounds.* For New Hampshire, the "C" code is also used to indicate those shelters at which tent camping also is permitted.

E   *"East,"* used to designate direction to facilities that are to the right of the Trail when traveling north (*i.e.,* toward Katahdin).

G   *Groceries, supplies.*

L   *Lodgings other than Trail shelters, campsites, and campgrounds:* for example, motels, hotels, cottages, and hostels. This code is also used for the Appalachian Mountain Club (AMC) huts in New Hampshire and camps (commercial cottages) in Maine.

m   *Miles.*

M   *Meals; restaurants.*

nw   *No potable water.* This is used in shelter and campsite listings only.

P.O.   *Post office.* Towns without post offices are listed only if the Trail goes directly through them; "P.O." is omitted in those cases.

R   *Road access.* Only roads open to the public and passable by ordinary automobiles are designated. Included are road crossings and locations where the Trail runs along a road or is adjacent to a road that provides access to the Trail. Where the road crossings are frequent (every two miles or less), lesser ones are omitted.

S   *Shelter.* A three-sided structure, with or without bunks or floors, intended as overnight housing for hikers (also known as lean-tos in some areas). Included in this category are unlocked cabins or lodges, found primarily in New Hampshire, Vermont, Pennsylvania, and Maryland. (See also "L".)

W   *"West,"* used to designate direction to facilities that are to the left of the Trail when traveling north (*i.e.,* toward Katahdin).

w   *Water* (from springs, streams, *etc.*). In general, where available, water sources are listed about every three to four miles. Other water sources do exist, and not every water source is listed in the *Data Book*. **Note: All water should be purified before use.**

✫   Indicates an **Appalachian Trail Community**, a town designated by the ATC as a participant in A.T. protection work through local education initiatives and land-conservation activity, while ATC helps it with "green tourism" development. A list of designated towns and counties can be found on page 87.

Appalachian Trail Distances

These sections and Trail points correspond to the beginnings and endings of chapters in this book and the eleven-volume series of official Appalachian Trail Guides.

Length by Section

Maine	281.8
New Hampshire–Vermont	311.7
Massachusetts–Connecticut	140.5
New York–New Jersey	162.0
Pennsylvania	229.2
Maryland–West Virginia–Northern Virginia	94.9
Shenandoah National Park	107.8
Central Virginia	226.1
Southwest Virginia	166.8
Tennessee–North Carolina	302.6
North Carolina–Georgia	166.4

Cumulative Distances

Miles from Katahdin		Miles from Springer Mountain
0.0	Baxter Peak, Katahdin, Maine	2,189.8
281.8	Maine–New Hampshire Line	1,908.0
593.5	Vermont–Massachusetts Line	1,596.3
734.0	Connecticut–New York Line	1,455.8
896.0	New Jersey–Pennsylvania Line	1,293.8
1,125.2	Pennsylvania–Maryland Line	1,064.6
1,220.1	Front Royal, Virginia	969.7
1,327.9	Rockfish Gap, Virginia	861.9
1,554.0	New River, Virginia	635.8
1,720.8	Damascus, Virginia	469.0
2,023.4	Fontana Dam, North Carolina	166.4
2,189.8	Springer Mountain, Georgia	0.0

GBS	N to S	Features	Facilities (see page 8 for codes)	S to N	Map

	N to S	Features	Facilities	S to N	
	0.0	Katahdin (Baxter Peak) (5,268')		281.8	
	1.0	Thoreau Spring	w	280.8	
	4.0	Katahdin Stream Falls	w	277.8	
	5.2	Katahdin Stream Campground, Birches Campsite (1,070') (C,S,w on A.T.)	CSw	276.6	
	5.3	Cross Tote Road	R	276.5	
	7.5	Daicey Pond Campground Road (L,w 0.1m E)	RLw	274.3	
	8.8	Big Niagara Falls	w	273.0	
	9.6	Upper Fork Nesowadnehunk Stream (ford)	w	272.2	
	10.5	Lower Fork Nesowadnehunk Stream (ford)	w	271.3	
	11.0	Pine Point	w	270.8	
	14.0	Katahdin Stream	w	267.8	
	14.4	Abol Stream, Baxter Park Boundary		267.4	
	15.1	Abol Bridge over West Branch of Penobscot River; junction with International A.T. (588') (C,G,w on A.T.)	RCGw	266.7	
	18.6	Hurd Brook Lean-to (710')	Sw	263.2	
	21.1	Rainbow Ledges (1,517')		260.7	
	22.9	Rainbow Lake (east end)	w	258.9	
	26.3	Rainbow Spring Campsite	Cw	255.5	
	28.1	Rainbow Lake (west end) Side Trail	w	253.7	
	30.1	Rainbow Stream Lean-to (1,020')	Sw	251.7	
	32.5	Pollywog Stream (682')	w	249.3	
	33.9	Crescent Pond (west end)	w	247.9	
	36.3	Nesuntabunt Mountain (1,520')		245.5	
	38.2	Wadleigh Stream Lean-to	Sw	243.6	
	40.8	Nahmakanta Lake (south end) (650')	Rw	241.0	

Maine Section 1

Maine Section 2

Maine A.T. Club

Maine Map 1

Maine

Miles from Katahdin — *Miles from Maine–N.H. Line*

N to S	Features	Facilities	S to N
42.5	Tumbledown Dick Trail		239.3
44.0	Nahmakanta Stream Campsite	Cw	237.8
46.0	Logging Road	R	
	(C,L,M 1m E)	RCLM	235.8
47.7	Pemadumcook Lake (southwest shore)	w	234.1
48.3	Potaywadjo Spring Lean-to (710')	Sw	233.5
50.1	Sand Beach, Lower Jo-Mary Lake	w	231.7
51.8	Antlers Campsite (500')	Cw	230.0
53.1	Mud Pond (outlet)	w	228.7
56.0	Jo-Mary Road		
	(w on A.T.; C,G 6m E)	RCGw	225.8
59.7	Cooper Brook Falls Lean-to (880')	Sw	222.1
62.0	Crawford Pond (outlet)	w	219.8
62.9	Kokadjo–B Pond Road	R	218.9
64.3	Little Boardman Mountain (1,980')		217.5
65.6	Spring	w	216.2
65.9	Mountain View Pond (outlet)	w	215.9
67.5	East Branch of Pleasant River (ford)	w	214.3
67.8	East Branch Lean-to (1,225')	Sw	214.0
69.8	West Branch Ponds Road		
	(L,M 4m W)	RLM	212.0
71.4	Logan Brook Lean-to (2,480')	Sw	210.4
72.8	White Cap Mountain (3,650')		209.0
73.9	White Brook Trail		207.9
74.5	Hay Mountain		207.3
76.1	West Peak		205.7
76.8	Sidney Tappan Campsite (2,425')	Cw	205.0
77.7	Gulf Hagas Mountain		204.1
78.6	Carl A. Newhall Lean-to (1,860')	Sw	203.2
82.1	Gulf Hagas Cut-off Trail	w	199.7

Maine A.T. Club — *Maine Section 3* — *Maine Map 2*

Maine

	N to S	Features	Facilities	S to N	
	Miles from Katahdin			*Miles from Maine–N.H. Line*	
Maine 3	82.8	Gulf Hagas Trail	w	199.0	Map 2
	83.8	The Hermitage (695')			
		(C,w 0.7m E)	Cw	198.0	
	84.1	West Branch of Pleasant River (ford)	w	197.7	
	84.6	Katahdin Iron Works Road	R	197.2	
	85.8	East Chairback Pond Side Trail (1,630')			
		(w 0.2m W)	w	196.0	
	88.0	Chairback Mountain (2,180')		193.8	
	88.5	Chairback Gap Lean-to (1,930')	Sw	193.3	
	88.9	Columbus Mountain (2,325')		192.9	
	90.2	West Chairback Pond Side Trail (1,770')	w	191.6	
	90.8	Third Mountain, Monument Cliff (1,920')		191.0	
	93.3	Fourth Mountain (2,380')		188.5	
Maine Section 4	95.4	Cloud Pond Lean-to Side Trail			Maine Map 3
		(S,w 0.3m E)	Sw	186.4	
	96.3	Barren Mountain (2,660')		185.5	
	99.4	Long Pond Stream Lean-to (940')	Sw	182.4	
	100.2	Long Pond Stream (ford) (620')	w	181.6	
	104.1	Wilson Valley Lean-to (1,045')	Sw	177.7	
	104.5	Montreal, Maine & Atlantic Railroad		177.3	
	104.8	Big Wilson Stream (ford) (600')	w	177.0	
	107.7	Little Wilson Stream	w	174.1	
	107.9	Little Wilson Falls		173.9	
	110.7	North Pond (outlet)	w	171.1	
	111.5	Leeman Brook Lean-to (1,060')	Sw	170.3	
	112.6	Lily Pond	w	169.2	
	113.3	Bell Pond	w	168.5	
	114.4	Spectacle Pond (outlet)	w	167.4	
	114.5	Maine 15 (1,215')	R	167.3	

Maine A.T. Club

Maine

Maine A.T. Club — Maine Section 5 — Maine Section 6 — Maine Map 4 — Maine Map 5

Maine

	N to S	Features	Facilities (see page 8 for codes)	S to N	
	Miles from Katahdin			*Miles from Maine–N.H. Line*	
	170.4	Campsite	Cw	111.4	
	171.4	Bog Brook Road, Flagstaff Lake (inlet)	Rw	110.4	
	171.5	East Flagstaff Road	R	110.3	
	172.9	Little Bigelow Lean-to (1,760')	Sw	108.9	
	174.6	Little Bigelow Mountain (east end) (3,010')		107.2	
	177.8	Safford Notch Campsite (2,230') (C,w 0.3m E)	Cw	104.0	
	177.9	Safford Brook Trail		103.9	
	179.8	Bigelow Mountain (Avery Peak) (4,090')		102.0	
	180.2	Avery Memorial Campsite, Bigelow Col, Fire Warden's Trail	Cw	101.6	
	180.5	Bigelow Mountain (West Peak) (4,145')		101.3	
	182.6	South Horn		99.2	
	183.1	Horns Pond Lean-tos (3,160')	CSw	98.7	
	183.3	Horns Pond Trail		98.5	
	185.0	Bigelow Range Trail, Cranberry Pond (w 0.2m W)	w	96.8	
	186.3	Cranberry Stream Campsite (1,350')	Cw	95.5	
	187.2	Stratton Brook (1,230')	w	94.6	
	187.4	Stratton Brook Pond Road	R	94.4	
	188.2	Maine 27; **Stratton, Maine, P.O. 04982** (P.O.,G,L,M 5m W)	RGLM	93.6	
	193.4	North Crocker Mountain (4,228')		88.4	
	194.4	South Crocker Mountain (4,040')		87.4	
	195.5	Crocker Cirque Campsite Side Trail (2,710') (w on A.T.; C 0.2m E)	Cw	86.3	
	196.5	Caribou Valley Road (2,220')		85.3	
	196.6	South Branch Carrabassett River (ford)	w	85.2	
	198.8	Sugarloaf Mountain Trail		83.0	
	200.9	Spaulding Mountain (4,000')		80.9	

Maine Section 7

Maine Section 8

Maine Map 5

Maine Map 6

Maine A. T. Club

Maine

GBS	N to S	Features	Facilities (see page 8 for codes)	S to N	Map
	Miles from Katahdin			*Miles from Maine–N.H. Line*	
	201.7	Spaulding Mountain Lean-to (3,140')	Sw	80.1	
	202.8	Mt. Abraham Trail		79.0	
	203.9	Lone Mountain (3,260')		77.9	
	207.0	Orbeton Stream (ford) (1,550')	w	74.8	
	209.7	Poplar Ridge Lean-to (2,960')	Sw	72.1	
	210.7	Stream	w	71.1	
	211.1	Saddleback Junior (3,655')		70.7	
	212.4	Redington Stream Campsite	Cw	69.4	
	213.1	The Horn (4,040')		68.7	
	214.7	Saddleback Mountain (4,120')		67.1	
	216.7	Eddy Pond	w	65.1	
	218.6	Piazza Rock Lean-to (2,065')	Sw	63.2	
	220.3	Sandy River (1,595')	w	61.5	
	220.4	Maine 4; **Rangeley, Maine, P.O. 04970**	☆		
		(P.O.,C,G,L,M 9m W)	RCGLM	61.4	
	222.5	South Pond (2,174')	w	59.3	
	225.2	Little Swift River Pond Campsite (2,460')	Cw	56.6	
	229.8	Sabbath Day Pond Lean-to	Sw	52.0	
	230.1	Long Pond (2,330')	w	51.7	
	231.9	Moxie Pond	w	49.9	
	233.5	Maine 17; **Oquossoc, Maine, P.O. 04964**			
		(P.O.,G,L,M 11m W)	RGLM	48.3	
	234.3	Bemis Stream (ford) (1,495')	w	47.5	
	238.1	Bemis Mountain Lean-to (2,800')	Sw	43.7	
	239.8	Bemis Range (West Peak) (3,580')		42.0	
	240.8	Bemis Stream Trail		41.0	
	244.0	Old Blue Mountain (3,600')		37.8	
	246.8	South Arm Road, Black Brook (ford) (1,410')			
		(w on A.T.; C,G 4.5m W)	RCGw	35.0	
	248.6	Moody Mountain (2,440)		33.2	

Maine A.T. Club — Maine Section 8 — Maine Section 9 — Maine 10 — Maine 11

Maine Map 6 — Maine Map 7

Maine

	Miles from Katahdin		Miles from Maine–N.H. Line	

GBS	N to S	Features	Facilities	S to N	Map
Maine 11	249.5	Sawyer Notch, Sawyer Brook (ford) (1,095')	w	32.3	
	250.9	Hall Mountain Lean-to (2,650')	Sw	30.9	
	252.2	Wyman Mountain (2,920')		29.6	
	255.1	Surplus Pond (outlet)	w	26.7	
Maine Section 12	256.9	East B Hill Road (1,485'); **Andover, Maine, P.O. 04216** (P.O.,C,G,L,M 8m E)	RCGLM	24.9	Maine Appalachian Trail Club
	257.7	Dunn Notch and Falls	w	24.1	
	261.4	Frye Notch Lean-to (2,280')	Sw	20.4	
	263.2	Baldpate Mountain (East Peak), Grafton Loop Trail (3,810')		18.6	
	264.1	Baldpate Mountain (West Peak) (3,662')		17.7	
	264.9	Baldpate Lean-to (2,660')	Sw	16.9	
	267.2	Grafton Notch, Maine 26 (1,495')	R	14.6	
	268.3	Brook	w	13.5	Maine Map 7
	270.7	Old Speck Trail, Grafton Loop Trail (3,985')		11.1	
	271.8	Speck Pond Campsite, Speck Pond Trail	CSw	10.0	
	272.7	Mahoosuc Arm (3,770')		9.1	
Maine Section 13	274.3	Mahoosuc Notch (east end) (2,150')	w	7.5	Appalachian Mountain Club
	275.4	Mahoosuc Notch (west end), Mahoosuc Notch Trail	w	6.4	
	276.4	Fulling Mill Mountain (South Peak) (3,395')		5.4	
	276.9	Full Goose Shelter and Campsite	CSw	4.9	
	277.9	Goose Eye Mountain (North Peak)		3.9	
	279.1	Goose Eye Mountain (East Peak) (3,790')		2.7	
	280.9	Mt. Carlo (3,565')		0.9	
	281.3	Carlo Col Trail, Carlo Col Shelter and Campsite (C,S,w 0.3m W)	CSw	0.5	
	281.8	Maine–New Hampshire Line (2,972')		0.0	

GBS	N to S	Features	Facilities (see page 8 for codes)	S to N	Map

	Miles from Maine–N.H. Line			*Miles from Vt.–Mass. Line*	
	0.0	Maine–New Hampshire Line (2,972')		311.7	
	1.9	Mt. Success (3,565')		309.8	
	4.7	Gentian Pond Shelter/Campsite (2,166')	CSw	307.0	
	5.4	Moss Pond	w	306.3	
	6.9	Dream Lake	w	304.8	
	9.6	Trident Col Tentsite (2,020')	Cw	302.1	
	10.7	Cascade Mountain (2,631')		301.0	
	15.0	Brook	w	296.7	
	16.2	Androscoggin River (750')	R	295.5	
	16.5	U.S. 2; **Gorham, N.H., P.O. 03581** (w on A.T.; P.O.,G,L,M 3.6m W; C,L,M 1.8m W)	RCGLMw	295.2	
	18.4	Rattle River Shelter	Sw	293.3	
	22.4	Mt. Moriah (4,049')		289.3	
	24.5	Imp Shelter/Campsite (3,250')	CSw	287.2	
	27.0	Middle Carter Mountain (4,610')		284.7	
	29.1	Zeta Pass (3,890')		282.6	
	30.5	Carter Dome (4,832')		281.2	
	31.0	Spring	w	280.7	
	31.7	Carter Notch, Carter Notch Hut (3,350') (L,M,w 0.2m E)	LMw	280.0	
	32.6	Wildcat Mountain, Peak A (4,422')		279.1	
	34.6	Wildcat Mountain, Peak D		277.1	
	37.6	Pinkham Notch, N.H. 16, Pinkham Notch Camp (2,050') (L,M,w on A.T.)	RLMw	274.1	
	39.7	Lowe's Bald Spot (2,860')		272.0	
	41.6	West Branch, Peabody River (2,300')	w	270.1	
	42.4	Osgood Tentsite	Cw	269.3	
	44.9	Mt. Madison (5,366')		266.8	

Left margin: *Appalachian Mountain Club* — N.H Section 1 — N.H. Section 2 — N.H. Section 3

Right margin: N.H.–Vt. Map 1 — N.H.–Vt. Map 2

New Hampshire–Vermont

GBS	N to S	Features	Facilities (see page 8 for codes)	S to N	Map
	Miles from Maine–N.H. Line			*Miles from Vt.–Mass. Line*	
	45.4	Madison Spring Hut, Valley Way Tentsite (C,w 0.6m W; L,M,w on A.T.)	CLMw	266.3	
	46.3	Thunderstorm Junction, Spur Trail to Crag Camp Cabin, Lowe's Path to Mt. Adams & Gray Knob Cabin (S,w 1.1m W, 1.2m W)	Sw	265.4	
	46.9	Israel Ridge Path to The Perch Shelter (C,S,w 0.9m W)	CSw	264.8	
	47.6	Edmands Col (4,938')		264.1	
	51.1	**Mt. Washington, N.H., P.O. 03589** (6,288') (P.O.,M on A.T.)	RM	260.6	
	52.5	Lakes of the Clouds Hut (5,012') (L,M,w on A.T.)	LMw	259.2	
	53.6	Mt. Franklin		258.1	
	54.2	Spring	w	257.5	
	55.5	Spring	w	256.2	
	56.4	Mt. Pierce (Mt. Clinton)		255.3	
	57.2	Mizpah Spring Hut, Nauman Tentsite (3,800') (C,L,M,w on A.T.)	CLMw	254.5	
	58.9	Mt. Jackson		252.8	
	60.3	Mt. Webster (3,910')		251.4	
	63.5	Saco River		248.2	
	63.6	Crawford Notch, U.S. 302, Dry River Campground (1,275') (C 1.8m E; M 1m W; C,G,L 3m E; L,M 3.7m W)	RCGLM	248.1	
	66.5	Ethan Pond Shelter/Campsite (2,860')	CSw	245.2	
	71.3	Zealand Falls Hut (2,630') (L,M,w on A.T.)	LMw	240.4	

N.H. Section 3 · N.H. Section 4

Randolph Mountain Club · Appalachian Mountain Club · N.H.–Vt. Map 2 · Map 3

New Hampshire–Vermont

GBS	N to S	Features	Facilities (see page 8 for codes)	S to N	Map
	Miles from Maine–N.H. Line			*Miles from Vt.–Mass. Line*	
	72.5	Zeacliff		239.2	
	75.5	Mt. Guyot, Guyot Shelter/Campsite (4,580') (C,S,w 0.8m E)	CSw	236.2	
	77.5	South Twin Mountain, North Twin Spur (4,902')		234.2	
	78.3	Galehead Hut (L,M,w on A.T.)	LMw	233.4	
	81.0	Garfield Ridge Shelter/Campsite (3,900')	CSw	230.7	
	81.4	Mt. Garfield (4,500')		230.3	
	84.9	Mt. Lafayette, Greenleaf Hut (5,260') (L,M 1.1m W; w 0.2m W)	LMw	226.8	
	85.9	Mt. Lincoln		225.8	
	86.6	Little Haystack Mountain		225.1	
	88.7	Liberty Spring Tentsite (3,870')	Cw	223.0	
	91.3	Franconia Notch, U.S. 3, Lafayette Place Campground (1,450'); **North Woodstock, N.H., P.O. 03262** (P.O.,G,L,M 5.8m E; G,L,M 2.2m E; C 2.5m W; L 1.6m E)	RCGLM	220.4	
	94.2	Lonesome Lake Hut (2,760') (L,M,w on A.T.)	LMw	217.5	
	96.1	Kinsman Pond Shelter/Campsite	CSw	215.6	
	96.7	North Kinsman Mountain		215.0	
	97.6	South Kinsman Mountain (4,358')		214.1	
	100.1	Eliza Brook Shelter/Campsite (2,400')	CSw	211.6	
	103.0	Mt. Wolf (East Peak) (3,478')		208.7	
	107.6	Kinsman Notch, N.H. 112 (1,870')	R	204.1	
	109.1	Beaver Brook Shelter (3,750')	Sw	202.6	
	111.4	Mt. Moosilauke (4,802')		200.3	
	116.0	Jeffers Brook Shelter (1,350')	Sw	195.7	

Left margin labels: N.H. Section 4 · N.H. Section 5 · Appalachian Mountain Club · N.H. 6 · DOC

Right margin labels: N.H.–Vt. Map 3 · Map 4

New Hampshire–Vermont

GBS	N to S	Features	Facilities (see page 8 for codes)	S to N	Map

Miles from Maine–N.H. Line

Miles from Vt.–Mass. Line

	N to S	Features	Facilities	S to N	
	117.1	N.H. 25 (1,000'); **Glencliff, N.H., P.O. 03238** (P.O.,L 0.5m E)	RL	194.6	
	119.5	Mt. Mist (2,200')		192.2	
	122.0	N.H. 25C (1,550'); **Warren, N.H., P.O. 03279** (w on A.T.; P.O.,G,M 4m E)	RGMw	189.7	
	124.6	Ore Hill	Cw	187.1	
	125.2	Cape Moonshine Road	R	186.5	
	126.8	N.H. 25A (900'); **Wentworth, N.H., P.O. 03282** (P.O.,G,L 4.3m E)	RG	184.9	
	130.1	Side trail to Mt. Cube (North Summit) (2,911')		181.6	
	131.7	Hexacuba Shelter (w on A.T.; S 0.3m E)	Sw	180.0	
	133.1	South Jacob's Brook (1,450')	w	178.6	
	137.0	Firewarden's Cabin (3,230')	Sw	174.7	
	137.1	Smarts Mountain Tentsite	Cw	174.6	
	140.8	Lyme–Dorchester Road	Rw	170.9	
	142.8	Dartmouth Skiway (880'); **Lyme, N.H., P.O. 03768** (P.O.,G,L,M 3.2m W)	RGLM	168.9	
	143.7	Trapper John Shelter (S,w 0.2m W)	Sw	168.0	
	144.2	Holts Ledge (1,930')		167.5	
	146.2	Goose Pond Road (952')	R	165.5	
	147.5	South Fork Hewes Brook	w	164.2	
	149.4	Moose Mountain Shelter	Sw	162.3	
	150.2	Moose Mountain (South Peak) (2,290')		161.5	

N.H. Section 7

N.H. Section 8

N.H. Section 9

N.H.–Vt. Map 4

N.H.–Vt. Map 5

Dartmouth Outing Club (DOC)

New Hampshire–Vermont

GBS	N to S	Features	Facilities (see page 8 for codes)	S to N	Map
		Miles from Maine–N.H. Line		*Miles from Vt.–Mass. Line*	
	151.8	Mink Brook	w	159.9	
	152.0	Three Mile Road	R	159.7	
	154.5	Etna–Hanover Center Road (845'); **Etna, N.H., P.O. 03750**			
		(P.O. 1.2m E)	R	157.2	
	155.9	Trescott Road	R	155.8	
	158.4	Ledyard Spring			
		(w 0.2m W)	w	153.3	
	158.9	Velvet Rocks Shelter			
		(S 0.2m W)	S	152.8	
	159.7	N.H. 120	R	152.0	
	160.4	Dartmouth College; **Hanover, N.H., P.O. 03755**	☆		
		(P.O.,G,L,M on A.T.)	RGLM	151.3	
	160.9	New Hampshire–Vermont Line, Connecticut River (400')	R	150.8	
	161.9	**Norwich, Vt., P.O. 05055**	☆		
		(P.O.,G,L,M 0.3m W)	RGLM	149.8	
	166.2	Happy Hill Shelter/Campsite (1,460')	CSw	145.5	
	168.8	Podunk Brook, Podunk Road	Rw	142.9	
	169.6	Tigertown Road, Podunk Road	R	142.1	
	170.2	Vt. 14, White River (400'); West Hartford, Vt.			
		(G,M on A.T.; P.O. 0.3m E)	RGMw	141.5	
	173.5	Joe Ranger Road	R	138.2	
	175.0	Thistle Hill Shelter	Sw	136.7	
	175.3	Thistle Hill (1,800')		136.4	
	177.3	Cloudland Road	R	134.4	
	179.1	Pomfret–South Pomfret Road	Rw	132.6	

Side labels: Dartmouth Outing Club (DOC) — N.H. Section 9; Green Mountain Club — Vt. Section 1; Vt. Section 2. Map: N.H.–Vt. Map 5

New Hampshire–Vermont

	N to S	Features	Facilities	S to N	
	Miles from Maine–N.H. Line		*Miles from Vt.–Mass. Line*		
Vt. 2	181.3	Woodstock Stage Road (820'); **South Pomfret, Vt., P.O. 05067** (w on A.T.; P.O.,G 0.9m E)	RGw	130.4	**N.H.–Vt. Map 5**
	183.5	Vt. 12 (882'); **Woodstock, Vt., P.O. 05091** (P.O.,G,L,M 4.4m E)	RGLM	128.2	
Vt. Section 3	187.3	Wintturi Shelter (1,900') (S,w 0.2m W)	Sw	124.4	
	189.7	Side trail to The Lookout		122.0	
	192.5	Chateauguay Road	R	119.2	
	197.2	Stony Brook Shelter (1,760')	Sw	114.5	
	201.5	River Road (1,214')	R	110.2	
	202.0	Thundering Brook Road	R	109.7	
	203.2	Kent Pond (L,M,w on A.T.)	RLMw	108.5	**Green Mountain Club**
	203.9	Vt. 100, Gifford Woods State Park	RCSw	107.8	
	205.3	Sherburne Pass Trail (2,440')		106.4	**N.H.–Vt. Map 6**
	206.2	Junction with Long Trail		105.5	
	207.2	U.S. 4 (1,880'); **Killington, Vt., P.O. 05751** (P.O.,G 2.2m E; L,M 0.9m E)	RGLM	104.5	
	209.1	Churchill Scott Shelter	CSw	102.6	
Vt. Section 4	211.0	Sherburne Pass Trail, Pico Camp (3,480') (S,w 0.5m E)	Sw	100.7	
	213.5	Cooper Lodge, Killington Peak Trail (3,900') (C,S,w on A.T.; M 0.2m E)	CMSw	98.2	
	217.8	Governor Clement Shelter (1,850')	Sw	93.9	
	219.4	Upper Cold River Road	Rw	92.3	
	220.2	Gould Brook (1,480')	w	91.5	

New Hampshire–Vermont

Miles from
Maine–N.H. Line

Miles from
Vt.–Mass. Line

	N to S	Features	Facilities	S to N	
	221.0	Cold River Road (Lower Road)	R	90.7	
	223.0	Lottery Road	R	88.7	
	223.4	Beacon Hill		88.3	
	223.9	Clarendon Shelter	CSw	87.8	
	224.9	Vt. 103 (860');			
		North Clarendon, Vt., P.O. 05759			
		(P.O. 4.2m W; M 0.5m W; G 1m W)	RGM	86.8	
	225.0	Clarendon Gorge, Mill River Suspension Bridgew		86.7	
	227.6	Minerva Hinchey Shelter (1,530')	CSw	84.1	
	231.2	Vt. 140 (1,160');			
		Wallingford, Vt., P.O. 05773			
		(w on A.T.; P.O.,G,L,M 2.7m W;			
		G 3.7m E)	RGLMw	80.5	
	231.3	Sugar Hill Road	R	80.4	
	232.7	Greenwall Shelter			
		(S,w 0.2m E)	Sw	79.0	
	233.2	Trail to White Rocks Cliff (2,400')		78.5	
	237.2	Green Mountain Trail to			
		Homer Stone Brook Trail		74.5	
	237.4	Spring	w	74.3	
	237.5	Little Rock Pond Shelter and Tenting Area	CSw	74.2	
	239.5	Danby–Landgrove Road (USFS 10),			
		Black Branch (1,500');			
		Danby, Vt., P.O. 05739			
		(P.O.,G,L,M 3.2m W)	RGLM	72.2	
	240.8	Big Branch Shelter	CSw	70.9	
	241.0	Old Job Trail to Old Job Shelter			
		(C,S,w 1m E)	CSw	70.7	
	242.5	Lost Pond Shelter	CSw	69.2	
	244.5	Baker Peak (2,850')		67.2	

Vertical labels (left margin): Green Mountain Club; Vt. Section 4; Vt. Section 5; Vt. Section 6

Vertical labels (right margin): N.H.–Vt. Map 6; N.H.–Vt. Map 7

New Hampshire–Vermont

	Miles from Maine–N.H. Line			*Miles from Vt.–Mass. Line*	
	246.5	Griffith Lake (north end)	w	65.2	
	246.7	Griffith Lake Tenting Area	Cw	65.0	
	247.2	Peru Peak Shelter	CSw	64.5	
Vt. Section 6	248.5	Peru Peak (3,429')		63.2	
	250.2	Styles Peak		61.5	
	251.8	Mad Tom Notch, USFS 21 (2,446'); **Peru, Vt., P.O. 05152** (P.O.,G 4m E; C 2.5m E)	RCGw	59.9	
	254.3	Bromley Mountain (3,260')		57.4	
	255.3	Bromley Shelter	CSw	56.4	
	257.3	Vt. 11 & 30 (1,840'); **Manchester Center, Vt., P.O. 05255** (P.O.,G,L,M 5.8m W; G 2.5m E; L,M 2.1m E, 2.7m E)	RGLM	54.4	N.H.–Vt. Map 7
	259.7	Spruce Peak		52.0	
	260.1	Spruce Peak Shelter	CSw	51.6	
	262.2	Old Rootville Road, Prospect Rock	R	49.5	
Vt. Section 7	263.1	Branch Pond Trail to William B. Douglas Shelter (S,w 0.5m W)	Sw	48.6	
	265.9	Winhall River	w	45.8	
	267.8	Stratton Pond, Lye Brook Trail to Stratton View Tenting Area (2,555') (w on A.T.; C,w 0.7m W)	Cw	43.9	
	268.0	Stratton Pond Trail, Stratton Pond Shelter	Sw	43.7	
	271.0	Stratton Mountain (3,936') (G,M 1.7m E)	GM	40.7	
	274.8	Stratton–Arlington Road (Kelley Stand Road) (2,230')	Rw	36.9	

Green Mountain Club

New Hampshire–Vermont

GBS	N to S	Features	Facilities (see page 8 for codes)	S to N	Map
			Miles from	*Miles from*	
	Miles from Maine–N.H. Line			*Vt.–Mass. Line*	
	278.4	Story Spring Shelter	CSw	33.3	
	279.3	South Alder Brook	w	32.4	
	283.0	Kid Gore Shelter, Caughnawaga Tentsites	CSw	28.7	
	287.0	Glastenbury Mountain (3,748')		24.7	
	287.3	Goddard Shelter	Sw	24.4	
	289.8	Glastenbury Lookout		21.9	
	291.6	Little Pond Lookout (3,060')		20.1	
	294.2	Hell Hollow Brook	w	17.5	
	295.8	Melville Nauheim Shelter	Sw	15.9	
	297.4	City Stream, Vt. 9 (1,360'); **Bennington, Vt., P.O. 05201** (P.O.,G,L,M 5m W; L 2.7m E; G 3.9m W)RGLMw		14.3	
	299.2	Harmon Hill (2,325')		12.5	
	301.7	Congdon Shelter	CSw	10.0	
	305.9	Roaring Branch	w	5.8	
	308.6	County Road	R	3.1	
	308.9	Seth Warner Shelter and Primitive Camping Area (C,S,w 0.2m W)	CSw	2.8	
	311.3	Brook	w	0.4	
	311.7	Vermont–Massachusetts Line, southern end of Long Trail (2,330')		0.0	

Vt. Section 8

Vt. Section 9

Green Mountain Club

N.H.–Vt. Map 8

Massachusetts–Connecticut

		Miles from Vt.–Mass. Line		*Miles from Conn.–N.Y. Line*	
Mass. Sec. 1	0.0	Vermont–Massachusetts Line, southern end of Long Trail (2,330')		140.5	AMC Berkshire Chapter
	0.8	Eph's Lookout		139.7	
	1.3	Pine Cobble Trail		139.2	
	2.3	Sherman Brook Primitive Campsite	Cw	138.2	
	4.1	Mass. 2 (650');			
		North Adams, Mass., P.O. 01247;	☆		
		Williamstown, Mass., P.O. 01267			
		(P.O.,G,L,M 2.5m E, 2.9m W; G 2.4m E; M 0.7m E; G,M 0.5m W; L 1.6m W)	RGLM	136.4	
	5.0	Pattison Road	Rw	135.5	
Mass. Section 2	7.1	Wilbur Clearing Shelter (2,300') (C,S,w 0.3m W)	CSw	133.4	Mass.–Conn. Map 1
	7.2	Notch Road	R	133.3	
	10.4	Mt. Greylock, Summit Road, Bascom Lodge (3,491') (L,M,w on A.T.)	RLMw	130.1	
	10.9	Notch Road, Rockwell Road	R	129.6	
	13.1	Jones Nose Trail		127.4	
	13.7	Mark Noepel Shelter (2,800') (C,S,w 0.2m E)	CSw	126.8	
	14.6	Old Adams Road		125.9	
	17.3	Outlook Avenue	R	123.2	
Mass. Section 3	18.1	Mass. 8 (1,000');			
		Cheshire, Mass., P.O. 01225 (G 0.2m W)	RG	122.4	
	18.6	Church Street, School Street (P.O., M, w on A.T.; L 0.1m W)	RLMw	121.9	
	20.0	The Cobbles		120.5	
	22.5	Gore Pond (2,050')		118.0	

Massachusetts–Connecticut

GBS	N to S	Features	Facilities (see page 8 for codes)	S to N	Map
	Miles from Vt.–Mass. Line			*Miles from Conn.–N.Y. Line*	
	22.9	Crystal Mountain Campsite (C,w 0.2m E)	Cw	117.6	
	26.6	Gulf Road	R	113.9	
	27.6	Mass. 8, Mass. 9 (1,200'); **Dalton, Mass., P.O. 01226** (M on A.T.; P.O.,G,L,M 0.3m W)	RL	112.9	
	28.2	CSX Railroad		112.3	
	30.3	Grange Hall Road	R	110.2	
	30.6	Kay Wood Shelter (S,w 0.2m E)	Sw	109.9	
	33.3	Warner Hill (2,050')		107.2	
	34.0	Blotz Road	R	106.5	
	35.2	Stream	w	105.3	
	37.2	Pittsfield Road (Washington Mountain Road); (G,L 4.6m E; M 1.8m E)	RGLM	103.3	
	38.7	West Branch Road	R	101.8	
	39.4	October Mountain Shelter (1,950')	CSw	101.1	
	41.2	County Road	R	99.3	
	43.5	Finerty Pond	w	97.0	
	45.3	Becket Mountain (2,180')		95.2	
	45.8	Tyne Road	R	94.7	
	46.6	U.S. 20 (1,400'); **Lee, Mass., P.O. 01238** (P.O.,G,L,M 5m W)	RGLM	93.9	
	46.9	Greenwater Brook	w	93.6	
	47.0	Massachusetts Turnpike		93.5	
	48.2	Upper Goose Pond Cabin (C,S,w 0.5m W)	CSw	92.3	
	49.0	Upper Goose Pond		91.5	
	50.9	Goose Pond Road	R	89.6	
	53.3	Webster Road (1,800')	Rw	87.2	

Left margin: AMC Berkshire Chapter — Mass. 3, Mass. Section 4, Mass. Section 5, Mass. Section 6

Right margin: Mass.–Conn. Map 1, Mass.–Conn. Map 2

Massachusetts–Connecticut

GBS	N to S	Features	Facilities (see page 8 for codes)	S to N	Map
			Miles from		
		Miles from Vt.–Mass. Line	Conn.–N.Y. Line		
	55.2	Tyringham Main Road (930')	R	85.3	
	56.3	Jerusalem Road	RLw	84.2	
		Tyringham, Mass., P.O. 01264			
		(P.O., L 0.6m W)			
	58.1	Shaker Campsite	Cw	82.4	
	58.4	Fernside Road			
		(w 0.2m W)	Rw	82.1	
	61.6	Beartown Mountain Road	Rw	78.9	
	62.2	Mt. Wilcox North Shelter (2,100')			
		(S,w 0.3m E)	Sw	78.3	
	64.0	Mt. Wilcox South Shelter	Sw	76.5	
	64.7	The Ledges		75.8	
	65.3	Benedict Pond			
		(C,w 0.5m w)	RCw	75.2	
	66.1	Blue Hill Road (Stony Brook Road)	R	74.4	
	67.3	Mass. 23 (1,000');			
		Great Barrington, Mass., P.O. 01230	☆		
		(P.O.,G,L,M 4m W)	RGLM	73.2	
	68.2	Lake Buel Road			
		(L,M 2.5m W)	RLM	72.3	
	69.3	Ice Gulch, Tom Leonard Shelter			
		(S on A.T.; w 0.2m E)	Sw	71.2	
	71.4	East Mountain (1,800')	w	69.1	
	72.8	Home Road	R	67.7	
	74.8	Housatonic River	R	65.7	
	75.7	U.S. 7; **Sheffield, Mass., P.O. 01257**			
		(P.O.,G,L,M 3.3m E; M 1.0m W, 0.8m E)	RGLM	64.8	
	77.5	Sheffield–Egremont Road (700')	R	63.0	

Mass. Section 7

Mass. Section 8

Mass.–Conn. Map 2

AMC Berkshire Chapter

Massachusetts–Connecticut

GBS	N to S	Features	Facilities (see page 8 for codes)	S to N	Map
	Miles from Vt.–Mass. Line			*Miles from Conn.–N.Y. Line*	
Mass. 9	79.3	Mass. 41 (Undermountain Road); **South Egremont, Mass., P.O. 01258** (P.O.,G,M 1.2m W)	RGM	61.2	
	80.2	Jug End Road (w 0.3m E)	Rw	60.3	
	81.3	Jug End (1,750')		59.2	
Mass. Section 10	83.0	Elbow Trail		57.5	
	83.6	Glen Brook Shelter	CSw	56.9	
	83.7	The Hemlocks Shelter	Sw	56.8	
	84.1	Guilder Pond Picnic Area	R	56.4	
	84.8	Mt. Everett (2,602')		55.7	
	85.5	Race Brook Falls Trail (C,w 0.4m E)	Cw	55.0	Mass.–Conn. Map 3
	86.6	Mt. Race		53.9	
	88.4	Laurel Ridge Campsite	Cw	52.1	
	89.3	Sages Ravine (1,340')	w	51.2	
	89.9	Sages Ravine Campsite	Cw	50.6	
	90.4	Massachusetts–Connecticut Line		50.1	
Conn. Section 1	91.1	Bear Mountain (2,316')		49.4	
	91.4	Bear Mountain Road		49.1	
	91.6	Riga Junction, Undermountain Trail		48.9	
	92.1	Brassie Brook (South Branch), Brassie Brook Shelter	CSw	48.4	
	92.7	Ball Brook Group Campsite	Cw	47.8	
	93.3	Riga Shelter	CSw	47.2	
	94.1	Lions Head (1,738')		46.4	
	96.3	Conn. 41 (Under Mountain Road); **Salisbury, Conn., P.O. 06068** (P.O.,G,L,M 0.8m W)	RGLM	44.2	
	97.0	U.S. 44 (700')	R	43.5	

AMC Berkshire Chapter · *AMC Connecticut Chapter*

Massachusetts–Connecticut

GBS	N to S	Features	Facilities (see page 8 for codes)	S to N	Map
	Miles from Vt.–Mass. Line		*Miles from Conn.–N.Y. Line*		
	99.8	Billy's View		40.7	
	100.6	Rand's View		39.9	
	100.7	Side trail to Limestone Spring Shelter (C,S,w 0.5m W)	CSw	39.8	
	101.4	Prospect Mountain (1,475')		39.1	
	102.7	Spring	w	37.8	
	103.2	Housatonic River Road	R	37.3	
	103.8	Housatonic River; **Falls Village, Conn., P.O. 06031** (P.O. 0.5m E)	R	36.7	
	105.7	Mohawk Trail (L,M 0.2m E)	LM	34.8	
	105.8	U.S. 7, Housatonic River (500')	R	34.7	
	106.4	U.S. 7, Conn. 112	R	34.1	
	106.8	Belter's Campsite	Cw	33.7	
	108.8	Hang Glider Vierw		31.7	
	109.6	Sharon Mountain Campsite	Cw	30.9	
	110.8	Mt. Easter (1,350')		29.7	
	111.1	Mt. Easter Road	R	29.4	
	112.0	Pine Swamp Brook Shelter	CSw	28.5	
	113.1	West Cornwall Road (800'); **West Cornwall, Conn., P.O. 06796** (P.O.,M 2.2m E)	RM	27.4	
	113.2	Carse Brook	w	27.3	
	115.4	Caesar Road, Caesar Brook Campsite	Cw	25.1	
	115.8	Pine Knob Loop Trail		24.7	
	116.5	Hatch Brook	w	24.0	
	117.7	Old Sharon Road	R	22.8	
	117.8	Guinea Brook	w	22.7	

Left margin: Conn. Section 2 | Conn. Section 3

Right margin: Mass.–Conn. Map 3 | AMC Connecticut Chapter

Massachusetts–Connecticut

GBS	N to S	Features	Facilities (see page 8 for codes)	S to N	Map
	Miles from Vt.-Mass. Line			*Miles from Conn.-N.Y. Line*	
Conn. Section 4	117.9	Conn. 4; **Cornwall Bridge, Conn., P.O. 06754** (P.O.,G,L 0.9m E)	RGL	22.6	Mass.–Conn. Map 4
	118.8	Silver Hill Campsite (1,000')	Cw	21.7	
	119.6	River Road, Spring	Rw	20.9	
	121.6	Stony Brook Campsite	Cw	18.9	
	122.0	Stewart Hollow Brook Shelter (400')	CSw	18.5	
	124.3	River Road	R	16.2	
	124.8	St. Johns Ledges		15.7	
	125.5	Caleb's Peak (1,160')		15.0	
	126.2	Skiff Mountain Road	R	14.3	
Conn. Section 5 (N.Y. Section 1)	129.0	Conn. 341, Schaghticoke Road (350'); **Kent, Conn., P.O. 06757** (P.O.,G,L,M 0.8m E)	RGLM	11.5	
	129.3	Mt. Algo Shelter	CSw	11.2	
	130.3	Thayer Brook	w	10.2	
	132.2	Schaghticoke Mountain Campsite	Cw	8.3	
	132.8	Indian Rocks		7.7	
	133.2	Connecticut–New York Line (1,250')		7.3	
	134.4	Schaghticoke Mountain		6.1	
	136.1	Schaghticoke Road	R	4.4	
	136.8	Side trail to Bulls Bridge Road Parking Area (R 0.2m E; G,M 0.4m E)	RGM	3.7	
	137.5	Ten Mile River (280')	Cw	3.0	
	137.7	Ten Mile River Shelter	Sw	2.8	
	138.7	Ten Mile Hill (1,000')		1.8	
	139.8	Conn. 55	R	0.7	
	140.5	Hoyt Road, Connecticut–New York Line (400'); **Wingdale, N.Y., P.O. 12594** (P.O.,G,M 3.3m W; M 1.5m W, 2.3m W)	RGM	0.0	

AMC Connecticut Chapter / *New York–New Jersey Trail Conference*

GBS	N to S	Features	Facilities (see page 8 for codes)		S to N	Map

Miles from
Conn.–N.Y. Line

Miles from
Delaware Water Gap, Pa.

	0.0	Hoyt Road, Connecticut–New York Line (400'); **Wingdale, N.Y., P.O. 12594** (P.O.,G,M 3.3m W; M 1.5m W, 3.3m W)	RGM	162.0
	1.0	Duell Hollow Road	R	161.0
	1.2	Wiley Shelter	Sw	160.8
	1.6	Leather Hill Road (750')	R	160.4
	6.7	Hurds Corners Road	R	155.3
	6.9	N.Y. 22, Metro-North Railroad, Appalachian Trail Railroad Station (480') (G 0.6m E; L 2.6m W; M 2.8m W)	RGLM	155.1
	9.3	County 20 (West Dover Road); **Pawling, N.Y., P.O. 12564** ☆ (P.O.,C,G,M 3.1m E; C 3.1m E)	RCGM	152.7
	10.0	Telephone Pioneers Shelter	Sw	152.0
	10.3	West Mountain (1,200')		151.7
	14.5	N.Y. 55 (720'); **Poughquag, N.Y., P.O. 12570** (P.O.,M 3.1m W; G 3.6m W; M 1.5m W; L 2.6m W)	RGLM	147.5
	14.8	Old Route 55	R	147.2
	16.7	Depot Hill Road	R	145.3
	17.8	Morgan Stewart Shelter	Sw	144.2
	17.9	Mt. Egbert (1,329')		144.1
	20.3	Stormville Mountain Road, I-84	R	141.7
	21.7	N.Y. 52 (800'); **Stormville, N.Y., P.O. 12582** (P.O. 1.7m W; G 0.5m E, 2.2m W, 2.4m W; G,M 2m E)	RGM	140.3
	23.3	Hosner Mountain Road	R	138.7

Side labels (left): N.Y. Section 2, N.Y. Section 3, N.Y. Section 4, N.Y. 5

Side labels (right): N.Y.–N.J. Map 1, *New York–New Jersey Trail Conference*

New York–New Jersey

Miles from Conn.–N.Y. Line

Miles from Delaware Water Gap, Pa.

	N to S	Features	Facilities	S to N	
	26.5	Taconic State Parkway	R	135.5	
N.Y. Section 6	26.8	Hortontown Road, RPH Shelter (350')	RSw	135.2	
	28.1	Shenandoah Tenting Area	Cw	133.9	
	29.2	Long Hill Road	R	132.8	N.Y.–N.J. Map 1
	29.6	Shenandoah Mountain (1,282')		132.4	
	33.8	N.Y. 301, Canopus Lake, Fahnestock State Park			
		(C,w 1m E)	RCw	128.2	
N.Y. Section 7	35.9	Sunk Mine Road (800')	R	126.1	
	37.5	Dennytown Road	RCw	124.5	
	40.2	South Highland Road	R	121.8	
	41.2	Canopus Hill Road (420')	R	120.8	
N.Y. 8	42.9	Old Albany Post Road, Chapman Road	R	119.1	
	43.7	Denning Hill (900')		118.3	
	45.6	Old West Point Road, Graymoor Friary	R	116.4	
	46.2	U.S. 9, N.Y. 403 (400'); **Peekskill, N.Y., P.O. 10566**			
		(P.O.,G,L,M 4.8m E; M 0.7m E; G on A.T.)	RGLM	115.8	
N.Y. Section 9	49.6	South Mountain Pass (Manitou Road)	R	112.4	N.Y.–N.J. Map 2
	49.8	Hemlock Springs Campsite	Cw	112.2	
	50.8	Camp Smith Trail, Anthony's Nose (700')		111.2	
	51.3	N.Y. 9D	R	110.7	
	52.0	Bear Mountain Bridge; **Fort Montgomery, N.Y., P.O., 10922**			
		(P.O.,G,L,M, 0.7m W)	RGLM	110.0	
N.Y. Section 10	52.1	Trailside Museum and Zoo (124')		109.9	
	52.8	Bear Mountain Inn, **Bear Mountain, N.Y., P.O. 10911**			
		(P.O. 0.3m E; L,M,w on A.T.)	RLMw	109.2	
	54.8	Bear Mountain (1,305')	Rw	107.2	

New York–New Jersey Trail Conference

New York–New Jersey

GBS	N to S	Features	Facilities (see page 8 for codes)	S to N	Map
	Miles from Conn.–N.Y. Line		*Miles from Delaware Water Gap, Pa.*		
	57.2	Seven Lakes Drive	R	104.8	
	59.0	Trail to West Mountain Shelter (S 0.6m E)	S(nw)	103.0	
N.Y. Section 10	59.9	Beechy Bottom Brook	w	102.1	
	60.1	Palisades Interstate Parkway (680')	R	101.9	
	60.8	Black Mountain (1,160')		101.2	
	62.2	William Brien Memorial Shelter	S(nw)	99.8	
	63.4	Goshen Mountain		98.6	
	64.2	Seven Lakes Drive	R	97.8	
	66.4	Arden Valley Road (1,196') (w 0.3m E)	Rw	95.6	
N.Y. Section 11	67.5	Fingerboard Shelter	S(nw)	94.5	
	68.5	Surebridge Mountain		93.5	
	69.6	Lemon Squeezer		92.4	
	70.2	Island Pond Outlet	w	91.8	
	71.5	Arden Valley Road	R	90.5	
	71.7	New York State Thruway (560')		90.3	
	71.9	N.Y. 17; **Arden, N.Y., P.O. 10910; Southfields, N.Y., P.O. 10975** (P.O. 0.7m W; P.O.,L,M 2.1m E; G 1.8m E, 5.7m E)	RGLM	90.1	
N.Y. Section 12	73.0	Arden Mountain (1,180')		89.0	
	73.7	Orange Turnpike (w 0.5m E)	Rw	88.3	
	74.4	Little Dam Lake		87.6	
	75.1	East Mombasha Road	R	86.9	
	75.9	Buchanan Mountain (1,142')		86.1	
	76.8	West Mombasha Road (G 0.6m W)	RG	85.2	
	78.0	Mombasha High Point (1,280')		84.0	

N.Y.–N.J. Map 2

New York–New Jersey Trail Conference

New York–New Jersey

GBS	N to S	Features	Facilities (see page 8 for codes)	S to N	Map

Miles from Conn.–N.Y. Line　　　　　　　*Miles from Delaware Water Gap, Pa.*

	80.0	Fitzgerald Falls	w	82.0	
	80.3	Lakes Road (680')	R	81.7	
	81.8	Wildcat Shelter	Sw	80.2	
	82.1	Cat Rocks		79.9	
	82.6	Eastern Pinnacles (1,294')		79.4	
	83.8	N.Y. 17A;			
		Greenwood Lake, N.Y., P.O. 10925			
		(G 1.6m W; P.O.,G,L,M 2m E;			
		G,L,M 3.5m W)	RGLM	78.2	
	89.4	Prospect Rock (1,433')		72.6	
	89.8	State Line Trail,			
		New York–New Jersey Line;			
		Hewitt, N.J., P.O. 07421			
		(P.O.,G,M 3.7m E)	GM	72.2	
	90.9	Long House Creek		71.1	
	92.0	Long House Road (Brady Road)			
		(G,M 0.7m W)	RGM	70.0	
	93.4	Warwick Turnpike (1,140')			
		(G 1.8m E, 2.7m W; L,M 0.8m W;			
		M 1.5m E)	RGLM	68.6	
	93.9	Wawayanda Shelter			
		(S on A.T.; w 0.4m E)	Sw	68.1	
	94.1	Wawayanda Road	R	67.9	
	94.7	Iron Mountain Road Bridge	R	67.3	
	95.8	Barrett Road;			
		New Milford, N.Y., P.O. 10959			
		(P.O.,G 1.8m W)	RG	66.2	
	97.5	Wawayanda Mountain (1,340')		64.5	

Left margin: *New York–New Jersey Trail Conference* — N.J. Section 1 — N.Y. Section 13 — N.Y. Section 12

Right margin: N.Y.–N.J. Map 2 — N.Y.–N.J. Map 3

New York–New Jersey

Miles from
Conn.–N.Y. Line

Miles from
Delaware Water Gap, Pa.

GBS	N to S	Features	Facilities (see page 8 for codes)	S to N	Map
	98.9	N.J. 94 (450'); **Vernon, N.J., P.O. 07462** (P.O.,G,M 2.4m E)	RGM	63.1	
	99.8	Canal Road	R	62.2	
	100.5	Pochuck Creek footbridge		61.5	
	101.2	County 517	R	60.8	
	102.7	County 565; **Glenwood, N.J., P.O. 07418** (P.O. 0.7m W; L 1m W)	RL	59.3	
	103.9	Pochuck Mountain (800')		58.1	
	105.4	Pochuck Mountain Shelter	S(nw)	56.6	
	105.9	Lake Wallkill Road (Liberty Corners Road)	Rw	56.1	
	108.2	Wallkill River	R	53.8	
	109.2	Oil City Road	R	52.8	
	109.7	N.J. 284 (420') (G 0.4m W)	RG	52.3	
	110.7	Lott Road; **Unionville, N.Y., P.O. 10988** (P.O.,G,M 0.4m W)	RGM	51.3	
	111.6	Unionville Road	R	50.4	
	113.9	Gemmer Road	R	48.1	
	116.5	County 519	R	45.5	
	117.8	High Point Shelter	Sw	44.2	
	118.3	Side trail to High Point Monument		43.7	
	119.5	N.J. 23 (1,500') (w on A.T.; G 2.5m E, 4.3m W; L 1.4m E, 4.4m W; M 4.3m W)	RGLMw	42.5	
	122.4	Trail to Rutherford Shelter (S,w 0.4m E)	Sw	39.6	
	124.8	Deckertown Turnpike	R	37.2	
	125.0	Mashipacong Shelter	S	37.0	

N.J. Section 2 · *N.J. Section 3* · *N.J. Section 4*

N.Y.–N.J. Map 3

New York–New Jersey Trail Conference

New York–New Jersey

Miles from Conn.–N.Y. Line — *Miles from Delaware Water Gap, Pa.*

New York–New Jersey Trail Conference

GBS	N to S	Features	Facilities (see page 8 for codes)	S to N	Map
N.J. 4	127.6	Crigger Road	R	34.4	Map 3
	128.4	Sunrise Mountain (1,653')	R	33.6	
	130.8	Trail to Gren Anderson Shelter	Sw	31.2	
	131.9	Culver Fire Tower		30.1	N.Y.–N.J. Map 4
N.J. Section 5	133.8	Culvers Gap, U.S. 206 (935'); **Branchville, N.J., P.O. 07826** (P.O. 3.4m E; G on A.T., 1.6m E; L 2.5m E, 1.9m W; M 0.1m W, 0.6m E)	RGLM	28.2	
	137.4	Brink Road Shelter (S,w 0.2m W)	Sw	24.6	
	139.6	Rattlesnake Mountain (1,492')		22.4	
	141.5	Buttermilk Falls Trail		20.5	
	144.4	Blue Mountain Lakes Road	Rw	17.6	
N.J. Section 6	148.3	Millbrook–Blairstown Road (1,260')	R	13.7	
	148.7	Rattlesnake Spring	w	13.3	
	149.3	Catfish Fire Tower (1,565')		12.7	
	151.7	Camp Road, Mohican Outdoor Center (C,L,w 0.3m W)	RCLw	10.3	
	156.0	Spring	w	6.0	
	156.1	Sunfish Pond (1,382')		5.9	
	157.4	Backpacker Site	C(nw)	4.6	
	159.0	Holly Springs Trail (w 0.2m E)	w	3.0	
	160.6	I-80 Overpass	R	1.4	
	161.0	Delaware Water Gap National Recreation Area Information Center	Rw	1.0	
	162.0	Delaware River Bridge (west end), New Jersey–Pennsylvania Line (350')	R	0.0	

Pennsylvania

	N to S	Features	Facilities	S to N	
		Miles from Delaware Water Gap, Pa.		*Miles from Pa.–Md. Line*	
	0.0	Delaware River Bridge (west end), New Jersey–Pennsylvania Line (350')	R	229.2	
	0.2	Pa. 611, **Delaware Water Gap, Pa., P.O. 18327** (P.O.,M 0.1m W; L,M 0.4m W; G,L 3.2m W)	☆ RGLM	229.0	
Pa. Section 1	0.9	Council Rock		228.3	Wilmington Trail Club
	1.7	Lookout Rock		227.5	
	2.7	Mt. Minsi (1,461')		226.5	
	4.7	Totts Gap		224.5	
	6.6	Kirkridge Shelter (1,500')	Sw	222.6	
	7.2	Fox Gap, Pa. 191	R	222.0	
	8.5	Wolf Rocks Bypass Trail (north end)		220.7	
	8.8	Wolf Rocks		220.4	
	9.3	Wolf Rocks Bypass Trail (south end)		219.9	
	15.7	Pa. 33 (980'); **Wind Gap, Pa., P.O. 18091** (P.O.,G,L,M 1m E; L 0.1m W)	☆ RGLM	213.5	
Pa. Section 2	16.7	Hahns Lookout		212.5	AMC Delaware Valley Chapter
	20.3	Leroy A. Smith Shelter (S 0.1m E; w 0.2m E)	Sw	208.9	
	23.8	Smith Gap Road	R	205.4	
	24.5	Spring (w 0.6m E)	w	204.7	
	26.3	Delps Trail (1,580')		202.9	
	31.1	Little Gap (1,100'); **Danielsville, Pa., P.O. 18038** (P.O.,G,M 1.5m E; w 1.2m W)	RGMw	198.1	
	36.1	Pa. 248	R	193.1	
	36.3	Lehigh River Bridge (east end), Pa. 873 (380'); **Palmerton, Pa., P.O. 18071** (P.O.,G,L,M 2m W)	RGLM	192.9	Keystone Trails Assn.

KTA Sections 1–6 Map

Batona

Pennsylvania

GBS	N to S	Features	Facilities (see page 8 for codes)	S to N	Map
		Miles from Delaware Water Gap, Pa.	*Miles from* Pa.–Md. Line		

GBS	N to S	Features	Facilities	S to N	Map
	36.4	Lehigh Gap, Pa. 873; **Slatington, Pa., P.O. 18080** (P.O.,G,L,M 2m E)	RGLM	192.8	
	37.0	George W. Outerbridge Shelter	Sw	192.2	
	41.4	Ashfield Road, Lehigh Furnace Gap (1,320'); **Ashfield, Pa., P.O. 18212** (P.O.,G 2.2m W; w 0.7m E)	RGw	187.8	
	43.8	Bake Oven Knob Shelter	Sw	185.4	
	44.4	Bake Oven Knob (1,560')		184.8	
	44.8	Bake Oven Knob Road	R	184.4	
	46.2	Bear Rocks		183.0	
	46.9	Knife Edge		182.3	
	47.9	New Tripoli Campsite (C,w 0.2m W)	Cw	181.3	
	49.7	Pa. 309, Blue Mountain Summit (1,360') (L,M,w on A.T.)	RLMw	179.5	
	51.9	Fort Franklin Road	R	177.3	
	53.8	Allentown Hiking Club Shelter	Sw	175.4	
	55.1	Tri-County Corner (1,560')		174.1	
	61.2	Hawk Mountain Road, Eckville Shelter (600') (S,w 0.2m E)	RSw	168.0	
	66.5	The Pinnacle		162.7	
	66.9	Trail to Blue Rocks Campground (C,G,S 1.5m E)	CGS	162.3	
	68.7	Pulpit Rock (1,582')		160.5	
	70.3	Windsor Furnace Shelter (940')	Sw	158.9	
	70.5	Windsor Furnace		158.7	

Left margin labels: KTA · Blue Mtn Eagle · Pa. Section 3 · Allentown Hiking Club · Blue Mountain Eagle Climbing Club · Pa. Section 4

Right margin label: KTA Sections 1–6 Map

Pennsylvania

GBS	N to S	Features	Facilities (see page 8 for codes)	S to N	Map
	Miles from *Delaware Water Gap, Pa.*			*Miles from* *Pa.–Md. Line*	
Pa. Section 4	73.1	Pocahontas Spring (1,200') (w on A.T.; L,M 1m E)	LMw	156.1	
	75.7	Pa. 61 (M 0.5m W)	RM	153.5	
	76.4	**Port Clinton, Pa., P.O. 19549** (400') (P.O. on A.T.; L,S 0.5m W; G,M,L 3m E)	RGLMS	152.8	
	80.4	Phillip's Canyon Spring (1,500')	w	148.8	
Pa. Section 5	83.1	Shartlesville Cross-Mountain Road; **Shartlesville, Pa., P.O. 19554** (P.O.,G,L,M 3.6m E)	RGLM	146.1	
	85.0	Eagle's Nest Shelter (S,w 0.3m W)	Sw	144.2	
	85.7	Sand Spring Trail (w 0.2m E)	w	143.5	KTA Sections 1–6 Map
	89.5	Black Swatara Spring (w 0.3m E)	w	139.7	
	90.8	Pa. 183, Rentschler Marker (1,440')	R	138.4	
	91.1	Fort Dietrich Snyder Marker (w 0.2m W)	w	138.1	Blue Mountain Eagle Climbing Club (BMECC)
Pa. Section 6	94.4	Shuberts Gap		134.8	
	94.5	Hertlein Campsite	Cw	134.7	
	97.0	Round Head and Shower Steps	w	132.2	
	99.6	Trail to Pilger Ruh Spring	Cw	129.6	
	100.1	Pa. 501; **Pine Grove, Pa., P.O. 17963,** 501 Shelter (P.O.,M 3.7m W; S,w 0.1m W; G 4.3m W; L 5.7m W)	RGLMSw	129.1	
	102.0	Pa. 645	R	127.2	
	104.2	Blue Mountain Spring, William Penn Shelter (1,380')	Sw	125.0	

Pennsylvania

GBS	N to S	Features	Facilities (see page 8 for codes)	S to N	Map
	Miles from Delaware Water Gap, Pa.			*Miles from Pa.–Md. Line*	
BMECC; Pa. Section 7	111.1	I-81	R	118.1	KTA Sections 7–8 Map
	111.5	Swatara Gap, Pa. 72 (480') (C,G,L,M 2m E)	RGL	117.7	
	112.9	Pa. 443; Green Point, Pa.	R	116.3	
Susquehanna A.T. Club	117.6	Rausch Gap Shelter (980') (S,w 0.3m E)	Sw	111.6	
	119.9	Cold Spring Trail		109.3	
	122.2	Yellow Springs Village Site		107.0	
	125.6	Stony Mountain; Horse-Shoe Trail (1,650')		103.6	
Pa. Section 8	128.9	Pa. 325, Clarks Valley (550')	Rw	100.3	
	129.2	Spring	w	100.0	
	131.5	Shikellimy Trail		97.7	
	132.9	Kinter View (1,320')		96.3	
	134.6	Victoria Trail		94.6	
	135.6	Peters Mountain Shelter	Sw	93.6	
	136.4	Table Rock		92.8	
York HC	138.4	Pa. 225	R	90.8	
	142.3	Clarks Ferry Shelter (1,260')	Sw	86.9	
	142.5	Campsite	Cw	86.7	
	144.7	U.S. 22 & 322, Norfolk Southern Railway	R	84.5	
Mtn. Club of Maryland; Pa. Section 9	145.3	Clarks Ferry Bridge (west end), Susquehanna River (380') (C on A.T.; M 0.1m W)	RCM	83.9	PATC Map 1
	145.5	Juniata River, Pa. 849	R	83.7	
	146.5	**Duncannon, Pa., P.O. 17020** (P.O.,L,M on A.T., G 0.6m W)	☆ RGLM	82.7	
	147.0	U.S. 11 & 15, Pa. 274	R	82.2	
	148.7	Hawk Rock		80.5	
	150.6	Cove Mountain Shelter (1,200')	Sw	78.6	
	155.6	Pa. 850 (650')	R	73.6	

Pennsylvania

GBS	N to S	Features	Facilities (see page 8 for codes)	S to N	Map

Miles from Delaware Water Gap, Pa.

Miles from Pa.–Md. Line

	N to S	Features	Facilities	S to N	Map
Pa. 9	157.9	Darlington Shelter (1,250')	Sw	71.3	MCM
	158.0	Darlington Trail, Tuscarora Trail		71.2	
	158.9	Spring	w	70.3	
	159.9	Pa. 944 (480'); Donnellytown, Pa.	R	69.3	
	161.9	Conodoguinet Creek, Scott Farm Trail Work Center	Rw	67.3	
Pa. Section 10	163.3	I-81 Crossing	R	65.9	
	164.2	U.S. 11; **Carlisle, Pa., P.O. 17013** **New Kingston, Pa., P.O. 17072** (P.O. 5m W; 1.7m E; G 1.3m E; L,M 0.3m W; M 0.3m E)	RGLM	65.0	Cumberland Valley A.T. Club
	165.4	Pennsylvania Turnpike	R	63.8	
	168.1	Trindle Road (Pa. 641)	R	61.1	PATC Map 1
	170.2	Pa. 74	R	59.0	
	172.2	Pa. 174, ATC Mid-Atlantic Regional Office; **Boiling Springs, Pa., P.O. 17007** (P.O.,w on A.T.; G,L,M 0.1m W; G 1m W)	☆ RGLMw	57.0	
Pa. Section 11	172.5	Yellow Breeches Creek (500')	R	56.7	
	172.7	Backpackers' Campsite	Cw	56.5	
	175.2	Center Point Knob (1,060')		54.0	
	176.1	Alec Kennedy Shelter	Sw	53.1	
	178.2	Whiskey Spring, Whiskey Spring Road	Rw	51.0	
Pa. 12	181.0	Pa. 94 (880'); **Mount Holly Springs, Pa., P.O. 17065** (P.O.,G,M 2.5m W)	RGM	48.2	Mtn. Club of Md.
	182.8	Hunters Run Road (Pa. 34); **Gardners, Pa., P.O. 17324** (P.O. 5m E; G 0.2m E)	RG	46.4	PATC 2–3

Pennsylvania

GBS	N to S	Features	Facilities (see page 8 for codes)	S to N	Map
			Miles from		
		Miles from *Delaware Water Gap, Pa.*	*Pa.–Md. Line*		
	183.7	Pine Grove Road (C,M 0.4m W)	RCM	45.5	
	184.2	James Fry (Tagg Run) Shelter (S,w 0.2m E)	Sw	45.0	
	185.4	Side trail to Mountain Creek Campground (C,G 0.7m W)	CG	43.8	
	185.6	Limekiln Road	R	43.6	
	188.9	Side trail to Pole Steeple (1,300')		40.3	
	191.4	Pine Grove Furnace State Park	RCGLw	37.8	
	191.7	Pa. 233 (900'), Appalachian Trail Museum	Rw	37.5	
	195.1	Toms Run Shelter (1)	Sw	34.1	
	196.2	Woodrow Road	R	33.0	
	198.1	Michener Cabin (locked) (w 0.3m E)	w	31.1	
	200.0	Shippensburg Road, Big Flat Fire Tower (2,040')	R	29.2	
	201.3	Birch Run Shelter	Sw	27.9	
	203.7	Milesburn Road, Milesburn Cabin (locked)	Rw	25.5	
	204.1	Ridge Road, Means Hollow Road	R	25.1	
	204.6	Middle Ridge Road	R	24.6	
	207.2	Sandy Sod Junction (1,980')	R	22.0	
	208.7	Quarry Gap Shelters	Sw	20.5	
	209.4	Quarry Gap Road	R	19.8	
	211.3	U.S. 30, Caledonia State Park, Thaddeus Stevens Museum (960'); **Fayetteville, Pa., P.O. 17222** (P.O.,G,L,M 3.5m W; C,w on A.T.; M 0.5m W; G 0.9m W)	RCGLMw	17.9	

Left margin: *Mountain Club of Maryland* / Pa. Section 12 / *Potomac A.T. Club* / Pa. Section 13

Right margin: PATC Maps 2–3

Pennsylvania

| --- | --- | --- | --- | --- | --- |
	Miles from Delaware Water Gap, Pa.			*Miles from Pa.–Md. Line*	
	214.3	Rocky Mountain Shelters (S 0.2m E; w 0.5m E)	Sw	14.9	
	216.0	Pa. 233 (1,600'); **South Mountain, Pa., P.O. 17261** (P.O.,G 1.2m E)	RG	13.2	
	216.3	Swamp Road	R	12.9	
	219.6	Chimney Rocks (1,900')		9.6	
	220.9	Tumbling Run Shelters, Hermitage Cabin (locked)	Sw	8.3	
Pa. Section 14	221.1	Old Forge Road (1,000')	R	8.1	PATC Map 4
	221.7	Rattlesnake Run Road	R	7.5	
	222.1	Antietam Shelter, Old Forge Park	RSw	7.1	
	224.5	Deer Lick Shelters (1,420')	Sw	4.7	
	225.8	Bailey Spring	w	3.4	
	226.4	Mackie Run, Mentzer Gap Road	R	2.8	
	226.6	Pa. 16; **Blue Ridge Summit, Pa., P.O. 17214** (P.O.,G,M 1.2m E; G 2.6m W)	RGM	2.6	
	226.9	Old Pa. 16	R	2.3	
	228.1	Buena Vista Road	Rw	1.1	
	229.1	Pen Mar Road	R	0.1	
	229.2	Pennsylvania–Maryland Line (1,250')	R	0.0	

Potomac A.T. Club

Maryland–West Virginia–Northern Virginia

GBS	N to S	Features	Facilities (see page 8 for codes)	S to N	Map

Miles from Pa.–Md. Line

Miles from Front Royal, Va.

	N to S	Features	Facilities	S to N	
	0.0	Pennsylvania–Maryland Line (1,250')	R	94.9	
	0.2	Pen Mar Park;			
		Cascade, Md., P.O. 21719			
		(P.O.,G,M 1.6m E; w on A.T.;			
		M 1.4m E)	RGMw	94.7	
	3.1	Trail to High Rock	R	91.8	
	4.9	Raven Rock Shelter	CSw	90.0	
		(C,S 0.2m W; w 0.1m E)			
	5.9	Raven Rock Hollow, Md. 491	R	89.0	
	6.7	Warner Gap Road	Rw	88.2	
	8.5	Foxville Road (Md. 77)	R	86.4	
	9.8	Ensign Cowall Shelter	Sw	85.1	
	10.0	Wolfsville Road (Md. 17) (1,400');			
		Smithsburg, Md., P.O. 21783			
		(P.O.,G,M 2.4m W; L 6.4m W)	RGLM	84.9	
	14.8	Pogo Memorial Campsite	Cw	80.1	
	15.4	Black Rock Cliffs (1,800')		79.5	
	16.4	Trail to Annapolis Rock			
		(C 0.2m W; w 0.4m W)	Cw	78.5	
	18.0	Pine Knob Shelter	CSw	76.9	
	18.6	I-70 Footbridge, U.S. 40			
		(C 1.4m W; M,w 0.5m W)	RCMw	76.3	
	19.4	Boonsboro Mountain Road	R	75.5	
	21.5	Washington Monument		73.4	
	21.9	Washington Monument Road	Rw	73.0	
	22.1	Monument Road	R	72.8	
	23.5	Turners Gap, U.S. Alt. 40 (1,000');			
		Boonsboro, Md., P.O. 21713			
		(M on A.T; P.O.,M 2.3m W;			
		G 1.6m W, 3.7m W)	RGM	71.4	

Potomac A.T. Club — Md. Section 1 · Md. Sec. 2 · Md. Section 3 · Md. Section 4 — PATC Maps 5–6

Maryland–West Virginia–Northern Virginia

GBS	N to S	Features	Facilities (see page 8 for codes)	S to N	Map
	Miles from Pa.-Md. Line			*Miles from Front Royal, Va.*	
Md. Section 5	23.7	Dahlgren Back Pack Campground	Cw	71.2	PATC Maps 5–6 *Potomac A.T. Club*
	24.5	Reno Monument Road	R	70.4	
	25.5	Rocky Run Shelter (C,S,w 0.2m W)	CSw	69.4	
	27.1	Lambs Knoll (1,600')		67.8	
	27.3	White Rocks Cliff		67.6	
	27.9	Trail to Bear Spring Cabin (locked) (w 0.5m E)	w	67.0	
	30.5	Crampton Gap Shelter (C,S,w 0.3m E)	CSw	64.4	
Md. Section 6	30.9	Crampton Gap, Gathland State Park, Gapland Road (Md. 572) (950'); **Burkittsville, Md., P.O. 21718** (P.O. 1.2m E; w on A.T.)	Rw	64.0	
	32.6	Brownsville Gap		62.3	
	34.6	Ed Garvey Shelter (S on A.T.; w 0.4m E)	Sw	60.3	
	36.7	Trail to Weverton Cliffs		58.2	
Md. Section 7	37.6	Weverton Road (G 1.4m W)	RG	57.3	
	37.8	U.S. 340 Underpass		57.1	
	38.0	Keep Tryst Road (L,M 1.2m W)	RLM	56.9	
	38.1	C&O Canal Towpath (east junction)		56.8	
	39.6	U.S. 340, Sandy Hook Bridge		55.3	
	40.7	C&O Canal Towpath (west junction)		54.2	
	40.9	Potomac River, Goodloe Byron Memorial Footbridge, Maryland–West Virginia Line (250')		54.0	

Maryland–West Virginia–Northern Virginia

GBS	N to S	Features	Facilities (see page 8 for codes)	S to N	Map
	Miles from Pa.–Md. Line		*Miles from Front Royal, Va.*		
	41.0	Shenandoah Street; Harpers Ferry National Historical Park (M 0.1m W)	RM	53.9	
	41.6	Appalachian Trail Conservancy Side Trail; **Harpers Ferry, W.Va., P.O. 25425** (P.O. 0.5m W; G 1.1m W; L 0.6m W; M 0.4m W; ATC 0.2m W)	☆ RGLM	53.3	
	41.9	U.S. 340, Shenandoah River Bridge (north end) (L 0.1m W; C 1.2m W)	RCL	53.0	
	42.6	Chestnut Hill Road (W.Va. 32)	R	52.3	
	43.3	Blue Trail to Loudoun Heights, West Virginia–Virginia Line (1,200')		51.6	
	47.2	Keys Gap, W.Va. 9 (G,M,w 0.3m W, 0.3m E)	RGMw	47.7	
	50.2	David Lesser Memorial Shelter (S 0.1m E; C,w 0.3m E)	CSw	44.7	
	53.4	Trail to Blackburn Trail Center (1,650') (C 0.1m E; S,w 0.3m E)	CSw	41.5	
	54.6	Wilson Gap		40.3	
	57.5	Devils Racecourse		37.4	
	57.6	Sand Spring	w	37.3	
	58.2	Crescent Rock		36.7	
	58.3	West Virginia–Virginia Line		36.6	
	58.6	Spring	w	36.3	

Potomac A.T. Club

W.Va.–Va. Section 1

W.Va.–Va. Section 2

PATC Map 7

Maryland–West Virginia–Northern Virginia

GBS	N to S	Features	Facilities (see page 8 for codes)	S to N	Map
	Miles from Pa.–Md. Line		*Miles from Front Royal, Va.*		
	60.8	Snickers Gap, Va. 7, Va. 679 (1,000'); **Bluemont, Va., P.O. 20135** (P.O. 1.7m E; G 1m W; M 0.3m W, 0.9m W)	RGM	34.1	
	61.4	Bears Den Rocks, Bears Den Hostel (L,w 0.2m E)	Lw	33.5	
	64.4	Sawmill Spring, Sam Moore Shelter	Sw	30.5	
	66.4	Spring	w	28.5	
	67.6	Morgans Mill Road (Va. 605)	R	27.3	
	71.3	Rod Hollow Shelter	Sw	23.6	
	74.9	Ashby Gap, U.S. 50 (900') (G,M 0.8m W; L 4m W; L,M 1.2m E)	RLM	20.0	
	77.5	Sky Meadows State Park Side Trail (C,w 1.3m E)	Cw	17.4	
	78.7	Spring	w	16.2	
	79.7	Whiskey Hollow Shelter (S,w 0.2m E)	Sw	15.2	
	82.3	Trillium Trail (1,900')		12.6	
	84.2	Manassas Gap Shelter	Sw	10.7	
	86.7	Va. 55 (800'); **Linden, Va., P.O. 22642** (P.O.,G 1m W)	RG	8.2	
	88.6	Va. 638	R	6.3	
	89.7	Jim & Molly Denton Shelter	CSw	5.2	
	91.6	Mosby Campsite, Tom Sealock Spring (1,800')	Cw	3.3	
	94.9	U.S. 522 (950'); **Front Royal, Va., P.O. 22630** (P.O.,G 4.2m W; G,M 3.2m W; L,M 3.6m W)	☆ / RGLM	0.0	

Va. Section 3 · Va. Section 4 · Va. Section 5 · PATC Map 8 · Potomac A.T. Club

GBS	N to S	Features	Facilities (see page 8 for codes)	S to N	Map

Miles from
Front Royal, Va.

Miles from
Rockfish Gap, Va.

	N to S	Features	Facilities	S to N
	0.0	U.S. 522 (950');		
		Front Royal, Va., P.O. 22630	☆	
		(P.O.,G 4.2m W; G,M 3.2m W;		
		L,M 3.6m W)	RGLM	107.8
	1.4	Va. 602	R	106.4
	2.9	Tom Floyd Wayside	Sw	104.9
	3.6	Possums Rest Overlook, SNP boundary; self-registration station for SNP camping permits		104.2
	3.8	Compton Gap Horse Trail		104.0
	5.3	Indian Run Spring		
		(w 0.3m E)	w	102.5
	5.6	Compton Gap; Skyline Drive, mile 10.4	R	102.2
	6.4	Compton Peak (2,909')		101.4
	6.8	Compton Springs	w	101.0
	7.7	Jenkins Gap; Skyline Drive, mile 12.3	R	100.1
	9.4	Hogwallow Gap;		
		Skyline Drive, mile 14.2 (2,739')	R	98.4
	10.0	Hogwallow Spring	w	97.8
	10.9	North Marshall Mountain (3,368')		96.9
	11.6	Skyline Drive, mile 15.9	R	96.2
	12.1	South Marshall Mountain (3,212')		95.7
	13.2	Gravel Springs Gap;		
		Skyline Drive, mile 17.7 (2,666')	R	94.6
	13.4	Gravel Springs Hut		
		(S,w 0.2m E)	Sw	94.4
	14.5	Skyline Drive, mile 18.9	R	93.3
	15.0	Little Hogback Mountain		92.8
	15.1	Little Hogback Overlook;		
		Skyline Drive, mile 19.7	R	92.7

Potomac A.T. Club

SNP Section 1 (Va. 6)

SNP Section 2 (Va. 7)

PATC Map 9

Shenandoah National Park

Miles from Front Royal, Va.

Miles from Rockfish Gap, Va.

	N to S	Features	Facilities	S to N	
	15.8	First peak of Hogback		92.0	
	15.9	Spring			
		(w 0.2m E)	w	91.9	
	16.1	Second peak of Hogback (3,475')		91.7	
	16.3	Skyline Drive, mile 20.8	R	91.5	
	16.4	Third peak of Hogback		91.4	
	16.6	Skyline Drive, mile 21.1	R	91.2	
	17.0	Tuscarora Trail		90.8	
	17.6	Rattlesnake Point Overlook; Skyline Drive, mile 21.9	R	90.2	
	18.3	Range View Cabin (locked) (w 0.1m E)	w	89.5	
	19.1	Elkwallow Gap; Skyline Drive, mile 23.9 (2,480') (G,M 0.1m E)	RGM	88.7	
	19.6	Spring	w	88.2	
	24.2	Byrds Nest #4 Picnic Shelter (0.5m E)	w	83.6	
	24.3	Beahms Gap; Skyline Drive, mile 28.5	R	83.5	
	24.6	Skyline Drive, mile 28.6	R	83.2	
	25.7	Pass Mountain (3,052')		82.1	
	26.5	Pass Mountain Hut (S,w 0.2m E)	Sw	81.3	
	27.7	Thornton Gap, U.S. 211; Skyline Drive, mile 31.5 (2,307')	R	80.1	
	29.6	Marys Rock (3,514')		78.2	
	30.2	Meadow Spring (w 0.3m E)	w	77.6	
	30.9	Byrds Nest #3 Shelter	S	76.9	
	31.9	The Pinnacle (3,730')		75.9	

SNP Section 2 (Va.7)

SNP Section 3 (Va.8)

PATC Map 9

PATC Map 10

Potomac A.T. Club

Shenandoah National Park

GBS	N to S	Features	Facilities (see page 8 for codes)	S to N	Map
	Miles from Front Royal, Va.		*Miles from Rockfish Gap, Va.*		
	32.9	Side trail to Jewell Hollow Overlook; Skyline Drive, mile 36.4	R	74.9	
	33.0	Pinnacles Picnic Ground; Skyline Drive, mile 36.7	Rw	74.8	
	35.2	Hughes River Gap; side trail to Stony Man Mountain Overlook; Skyline Drive, mile 38.6 (3,097')	Rw	72.6	
	36.8	Side trail to Stony Man summit		71.0	
	37.2	Skyland Service Road (north) (L,M 0.3m W)	RLM	70.6	
	38.0	Skyland Service Road (south)	R	69.8	
	40.1	Side trail to Crescent Rock Overlook; Skyline Drive, mile 44.4	R	67.7	
	40.5	Hawksbill Gap; Skyline Drive, mile 45.6 (3,361')	R	67.3	
	41.5	Side trail to Hawksbill Mountain, Byrd's Nest #2 Picnic Shelter (0.9m E)		66.3	
	41.8	Rock Spring Cabin (locked) & Hut (S,w 0.2m W)	Sw	66.0	
	43.7	Fishers Gap; Skyline Drive, mile 49.3	R	64.1	
	44.7	David Spring	w	63.1	
	45.3	Big Meadows (3,500') (C,L,M 0.1m E)	RCLM	62.5	
	46.2	Big Meadows Wayside, Harry F. Byrd, Sr., Visitor Center (w on A.T.; G,M 0.4m E)	RGMw	61.6	
	47.0	Spring	w	60.8	
	47.9	Milam Gap; Skyline Drive, mile 52.8	R	59.9	
	49.8	Hazeltop (3,812')		58.0	

Left margin labels: Potomac A.T. Club — SNP Section 3 (Va.8), SNP Section 4 (Va.9), SNP Section 5 (Va.10)

Right margin label: PATC Map 10

Shenandoah National Park

GBS	N to S	Features	Facilities (see page 8 for codes)	S to N	Map
			Miles from		
	Miles from Front Royal, Va.		*Rockfish Gap, Va.*		
	50.7	Bootens Gap; Skyline Drive, mile 55.1 (3,243')	R	57.1	
SNP Section 5 (Va. 10)	53.3	Bearfence Mountain Hut (S,w 0.1m E)	Sw	54.5	PATC Map 10
	54.0	Lewis Mountain Campground; Skyline Drive, mile 57.6 (C,G,L,w 0.1m W)	RCGLw	53.8	
	55.7	Spring	w	52.1	
	56.0	Pocosin Cabin (locked)	w	51.8	
	59.3	South River Picnic Grounds (w 0.1m W)	w	48.5	
SNP Section 6 (Va. 11)	62.3	Swift Run Gap, U.S. 33; Skyline Drive, mile 65.5 (2,367')	R	45.5	PATC Map 11
	63.6	Skyline Drive, mile 66.7	R	44.2	
	65.1	Hightop Mountain (3,587')		42.7	
	65.2	Spring	w	42.6	
	65.7	Hightop Hut (S 0.1m W; w 0.2m W)	Sw	42.1	
	66.9	Smith Roach Gap; Skyline Drive, mile 68.6	R	40.9	
	68.1	Little Roundtop Mountain		39.7	
	68.5	Powell Gap; Skyline Drive, mile 69.9 (2,294')	R	39.3	
SNP Section 7 (Va. 12)	71.8	Simmons Gap; Skyline Drive, mile 73.2	Rw	36.0	
	73.7	Pinefield Gap; Skyline Drive, mile 75.2	R	34.1	
	73.9	Pinefield Hut	Sw	33.9	
	75.5	Ivy Creek Overlook; Skyline Drive, mile 77.5	R	32.3	
	77.6	Spring (w 0.1m W)	w	30.2	

Potomac A.T. Club

Shenandoah National Park

GBS	N to S	Features	Facilities (see page 8 for codes)	S to N	Map
		Miles from Front Royal, Va.	*Miles from Rockfish Gap, Va.*		
	79.7	Loft Mountain Campground (3,300') (C,G,M,w 0.2m W)	CGMw	28.1	
	81.8	Doyles River Cabin (locked); Skyline Drive, mile 81.1 (w 0.3m E)	Rw	26.0	
	82.7	Doyles River Parking Overlook; Skyline Drive, mile 81.9	R	25.1	
	83.1	Skyline Drive, mile 82.2	R	24.7	
	84.0	Browns Gap; Skyline Drive, mile 82.9 (2,600')	R	23.8	
	85.5	Skyline Drive, mile 84.3	R	22.3	
	86.5	Blackrock (3,100')		21.3	
	87.1	Blackrock Hut (S,w 0.2m E)	Sw	20.7	
	87.6	Skyline Drive, mile 87.2	R	20.2	
	87.8	Blackrock Gap; Skyline Drive, mile 87.4 (2,321')	R	20.0	
	89.6	Skyline Drive, mile 88.9	R	18.2	
	93.7	Skyline Drive, mile 92.4 (3,100')	R	14.1	
	95.7	Turk Gap; Skyline Drive, mile 94.1	R	12.1	
	97.3	Skyline Drive, mile 95.3	R	10.5	
	98.9	Spring	w	8.9	
	99.1	Jarman Gap; Skyline Drive, mile 96.9; SNP southern boundary (2,173')	R	8.7	
	99.5	Spring	w	8.3	
	100.1	Calf Mountain Shelter (w 0.2m W; S 0.3m W)	Sw	7.7	
	102.3	Beagle Gap; Skyline Drive, mile 99.5	R	5.5	
	102.8	Bear Den Mountain (2,885')		5.0	
	104.1	McCormick Gap; Skyline Drive, mile 102.1	R	3.7	

Side labels: Potomac A.T. Club — SNP Section 7 (Va.12), SNP Section 8 (Va.13), SNP Section 9 (Va.14) — PATC Map 11

Shenandoah National Park

	Miles from Front Royal, Va.		Miles from Rockfish Gap, Va.		
SNP Sec. 9 (Va.14)	107.0	Self-registration for SNP camping permits, park entrance station (0.2m W)		0.8	**PATC Map 11** *Potomac A.T. Club*
	107.5	Skyline Drive, mile 105.2	R	0.3	
	107.7	I-64 Overpass		0.1	
	107.8	Rockfish Gap, U.S. 250, I-64 (1,902'); **Waynesboro, Va., P.O. 22980** (P.O.,G,L,M 4.5m W; G,L,M on A.T.)	☆ RGLM	0.0	

GBS	N to S	Features	Facilities (see page 8 for codes)	S to N	Map
	Miles from Rockfish Gap, Va.			*Miles from New River, Va.*	
Old Dominion A.T. Club / Va. Section 15	0.0	Rockfish Gap, U.S. 250, I-64 (1,902'); **Waynesboro, Va., P.O. 22980** (P.O.,G,L,M 4.5m W)	☆ RGLM	226.1	Central Va. Map 1
	5.0	Mill Creek, Paul C. Wolfe Shelter	Sw	221.1	
	6.5	Side trail to Humpback Visitors Center (w 1.3m W)	w	219.6	
	6.8	Glass Hollow Overlook		219.3	
	9.0	Bear Spring	w	217.1	
	10.5	Side trail to Humpback Rocks		215.6	
	11.5	Humpback Mountain (3,606')		214.6	
	14.3	Dripping Rock Parking Area; Blue Ridge Parkway, mile 9.6	Rw	211.8	
	14.8	Cedar Cliffs		211.3	
	18.6	Three Ridges Overlook; Blue Ridge Parkway, mile 13.1	R	207.5	
Tidewater A.T. Club / Va. Section 16	19.1	Reids Gap (2,645'), Va. 664; Blue Ridge Parkway, mile 13.6	R	207.0	
	20.8	Maupin Field Shelter	Sw	205.3	
	22.8	Hanging Rock		203.3	
	23.3	Three Ridges Mountain (3,970')		202.8	
	25.0	Chimney Rocks		201.1	
	27.0	Harpers Creek Shelter	Sw	199.1	
	29.7	Tye River	Cw	196.4	
NBATC / Va. Section 17	29.8	Va. 56 (997') (C,G 5m W)	RCG	196.3	
	31.1	Cripple Creek	w	195.0	
	34.1	The Priest (4,063')		192.0	
	34.6	The Priest Shelter	Sw	191.5	

Central Virginia

GBS	N to S	Features	Facilities (see page 8 for codes)	S to N	Map
		Miles from *Rockfish Gap, Va.*		*Miles from* *New River, Va.*	
Va. 17	35.5	Crabtree Farm Road (Va. 826), Crabtree Falls Trail (C,w 0.5m W)	RCw	190.6	
	36.3	Cash Hollow Road (3,280')	R	189.8	
	37.6	Cash Hollow Rock		188.5	
	38.4	Spy Rock		187.7	
	38.9	Spy Rock Road (3,454'); **Montebello, Va., P.O. 24464** (P.O. 2.5m W; C,G,L 2.2m W)	RCGL	187.2	
Va. Section 18	40.1	Porters Field	Cw	186.0	
	41.2	Seeley-Woodworth Shelter	Sw	184.9	
	41.9	Elk Pond Branch	Cw	184.2	
	43.1	North Fork of Piney River	Cw	183.0	Central Va. Map 1
	45.0	Greasy Spring Road	R	181.1	
	45.5	USFS 246	R	180.6	
	46.7	Salt Log Gap (north), USFS 63 (3,290')	R	179.4	
	48.0	Tar Jacket Ridge (3,840')		178.1	
Va. Section 19	48.9	Hog Camp Gap, USFS 48 (3,485')	RCw	177.2	
	50.2	Cole Mountain (4,022')		175.9	
	51.4	Old Hotel Trail, Cow Camp Gap Shelter (3,428') (S,w 0.6m E)	Sw	174.7	
	52.4	Bald Knob (4,059')		173.7	
Va. Section 20	55.2	Long Mountain Wayside, U.S. 60 (2,060'); **Buena Vista, Va., P.O. 24416** (P.O.,C,G,L,M 9.3m W)	☆ RCGLM	170.9	
	57.0	Brown Mountain Creek Shelter	Sw	169.1	
	59.0	Swapping Camp Road (USFS 38)	R	167.1	
	61.9	Pedlar River Bridge	w	164.2	Map 2
	62.0	USFS 39	R	164.1	

Natural Bridge A.T. Club

Central Virginia

*Miles from
Rockfish Gap, Va.*

*Miles from
New River, Va.*

	N to S	Features	Facilities	S to N
	63.9	Rice Mountain (2,169')		162.2
	65.8	Robinson Gap Road (Va. 607)	R	160.3
	66.1	Blue Ridge Parkway, mile 51.7; Punchbowl Mountain Crossing (2,170')	Rw	160.0
	66.5	Punchbowl Shelter (S,w 0.2m W)	Sw	159.6
	67.0	Punchbowl Mountain		159.1
	68.1	Bluff Mountain (3,391')		158.0
	69.6	Saltlog Gap (south) (2,573')		156.5
	70.7	Saddle Gap, Saddle Gap Trail		155.4
	72.2	Big Rocky Row (2,974')		153.9
	73.2	Fullers Rocks, Little Rocky Row (2,486')		152.9
	73.3	Rocky Row Trail		152.8
	75.3	Johns Hollow Shelter	Sw	150.8
	75.9	Va. 812 (USFS 36)	R	150.2
	76.0	Rocky Row Run (760')	Cw	150.1
	76.9	Lower Rocky Row Run bridge	w	149.2
	77.0	U.S. 501, Va. 130; **Big Island, Va., P.O. 24526; Glasgow, Va., P.O. 24555** (P.O.,G,M 5.6m E; P.O.,G,C,M 5.9m W; C,L 4.4m E)	☆ RCGLM	149.1
	77.2	James River Foot Bridge (678')		148.9
	78.4	Campsite	Cw	147.7
	79.2	Matts Creek Shelter	Sw	146.9
	81.1	Big Cove Branch	w	145.0
	81.9	Sulphur Spring Trail (north crossing) (2,588')		144.2
	82.4	Hickory Stand, Gunter Ridge Trail		143.7
	84.2	Sulphur Spring Trail (south crossing)		141.9

Va. Section 21

Va. Section 22

Natural Bridge A.T. Club

Central Va. Map 2

Central Virginia

GBS	N to S	Features	Facilities (see page 8 for codes)	S to N	Map
	Miles from Rockfish Gap, Va.			*Miles from New River, Va.*	
	84.7	Marble Spring	Cw	141.4	
	85.7	Highcock Knob (3,054')		140.4	
	86.9	Petites Gap, USFS 35;			
		Blue Ridge Parkway, mile 71.0 (2,369')	R	139.2	
	88.3	Harrison Ground Spring	w	137.8	
	90.2	Thunder Ridge Overlook;			
		Blue Ridge Parkway, mile 74.7 (3,525')	R	135.9	
Va. Section 23	90.6	Lower Blue Ridge Parkway crossing, mile 74.9	R	135.5	
	91.6	Thunder Hill Shelter	Sw	134.5	
	91.9	Upper Blue Ridge Parkway crossing, mile 76.3	R	134.2	
	92.5	The Guillotine		133.6	
	92.8	Apple Orchard Mountain (4,206')		133.3	Central Va. Map 2
	94.2	Parkers Gap Road (USFS 812); Blue Ridge Parkway, mile 78.4 (3,410')	R	131.9	
Va. Section 24	94.3	Apple Orchard Falls Trail		131.8	Natural Bridge A.T. Club
	96.0	Black Rock		130.1	
	96.9	Cornelius Creek Shelter	Sw	129.2	
	97.5	Floyd Mountain (3,560')		128.6	
	101.8	Bryant Ridge Shelter (1,330')	Sw	124.3	
	104.0	Fork Mountain (2,042')		122.1	
Va. Section 25	105.6	Va. 614, Jennings Creek (987') (w 0.3m E; C,G,L,M 1.6m E, L,M 4.5m W)	RCGLMw	120.5	
	107.1	Buchanan Trail		119.0	
	108.8	Cove Mountain Shelter	S(nw)	117.3	
	110.2	Little Cove Mountain Trail		115.9	
	110.6	Cove Mountain (2,707')		115.5	

Central Virginia

Miles from Rockfish Gap, Va. / *Miles from New River, Va.*

N to S	Features	Facilities	S to N
112.2	Bearwallow Gap, Va. 43, Blue Ridge Parkway, mile 90.9 (2,228'); **Buchanan, Va., P.O. 24066** (P.O.,G,M 5m W; L,M 7m W; C,L,M 4.9m E)	RCGLM	113.9
113.9	Blue Ridge Parkway, mile 91.8; Mills Gap Overlook	R	112.2
114.6	Blue Ridge Parkway, mile 92.5; Peaks of Otter Overlook	R	111.5
115.3	Bobblets Gap Shelter (S,w 0.2m W)	Sw	110.8
117.7	Blue Ridge Parkway, mile 95.3; Harveys Knob Overlook	R	108.4
118.3	Blue Ridge Parkway, mile 95.9; Montvale Overlook	R	107.8
119.4	Blue Ridge Parkway, mile 97.0; Taylors Mountain Overlook	R	106.7
120.2	Black Horse Gap, Old Fincastle Road (USFS 186); Blue Ridge Parkway, mile 97.7 (2,402')	R	105.9
122.2	Spring	w	103.9
122.6	Wilson Creek Shelter	Sw	103.5
123.3	Wilson Creek	w	102.8
125.2	Curry Creek	w	100.9
126.0	Salt Pond Road (USFS 191)	R	100.1
128.8	Fullhardt Knob Shelter (2,676')	Sw	97.3
131.8	Va. 652 (Mountain Pass Road)	R	94.3
132.3	Norfolk Southern Railway, U.S. 11; **Troutville, Va., P.O. 24175** (P.O.,G 0.8m W)	☆ RG	93.8

Va. Section 26 — Natural Bridge A.T. Club
Roanoke A.T. Club — Va. Section 27
Central Va. Map 2 / Central Va. Map 3

Central Virginia

Central Virginia

GBS	N to S	Features	Facilities	S to N	Map
	Miles from Rockfish Gap, Va.		*Miles from New River, Va.*		
Va. Section 29	166.2	Pickle Branch Shelter (S,w 0.3m E)	Sw	59.9	Cen. Va. Map 3
	167.4	Trout Creek, Va. 620 (Miller Cove Road) (1,525')	R	58.7	
	171.2	Audie Murphy Monument (3,100')		54.9	
	175.0	Craig Creek Valley, Va. 621 (1,560')	R	51.1	
Va. Section 30	176.3	Niday Shelter	Sw	49.8	
	177.0	Cabin Branch	Cw	49.1	
	178.7	Sinking Creek Mountain (3,490')		47.4	
	182.3	Sarver Hollow Shelter (S,w 0.4m E)	Sw	43.8	
	185.4	Va. 630, Sinking Creek (2,100')	Rw	40.7	
Va. Section 31	186.3	Sinking Creek Valley, Va. 42	R	39.8	
	187.7	Spring	w	38.4	
	188.7	Laurel Creek Shelter	Sw	37.4	
	191.7	Rocky Gap, Va. 601	R	34.4	
	192.7	Stream	w	33.4	Central Va. Map 4
	193.7	Johns Creek Valley, USFS 156 (2,102')	Rw	32.4	
	194.5	War Spur Shelter	Sw	31.6	
	198.2	Campsites, spring	Cw	27.9	
	199.4	Wind Rock (4,121')		26.7	
Va. Section 32	199.6	Mountain Lake Road/ Salt Sulphur Turnpike (Va. 613)	R	26.5	
	203.3	Bailey Gap Shelter	S	22.8	
	203.5	Spring	w	22.6	
	204.8	Va. 635 (Big Stony Creek Road), Stony Creek (2,450')	R	21.3	
	205.8	Dismal Branch	w	20.3	
	206.9	Va. 635 (Big Stony Creek Road), Stony Creek Valley	R	19.2	
	207.2	Pine Swamp Branch Shelter	Sw	18.9	

Roanoke A.T. Club (RATC)

Central Virginia

GBS	N to S	Features	Facilities (see page 8 for codes)	S to N	Map
	Miles from Rockfish Gap, Va.			*Miles from New River, Va.*	
	209.7	Allegheny Trail		16.4	
	209.9	Peters Mountain (3,860')		16.2	
	212.1	Dickenson Gap		14.0	
	213.7	Groundhog Trail		12.4	
	214.7	Symms Gap Meadow		11.4	
Va. Section 33	218.2	Campsite, spring	Cw	7.9	Central Va. Map 4
	219.8	Rice Field Shelter (3,400')		6.3	
	220.0	Spring	w	6.1	
	221.1	Stream	w	5.0	
	222.2	Clendennin Road (Va. 641)	R	3.9	
	222.7	Hemlock Ridge		3.4	
	226.1	U.S. 460, Senator Shumate Bridge (east end), New River (1,600') (G 0.1m E)	RG	0.0	

Outdoor Club of Virginia Tech

GBS	N to S	Features	Facilities (see page 8 for codes)	S to N	Map

	Miles from New River, Va.			*Miles from Damascus, Va.*	
	0.0	U.S. 460, Senator Shumate Bridge (east end), New River (1,600')	R	166.8	
	0.4	Va. 100, **Pearisburg, Va., P.O. 24134** (P.O.,G,L,M 1.3m E)	☆ RGLM	166.4	
	1.4	Va. 634	R	165.4	
	3.4	Angels Rest, Pearis Mountain (3,550')		163.4	
	3.9	Campsite, spring	Cw	162.9	
	9.8	Doc's Knob Shelter	Sw	157.0	
	12.1	Sugar Run Gap, Sugar Run Gap Road (Va. 663) (L 0.5m E)	RL	154.7	
	13.7	Big Horse Gap, USFS 103 (3,752')	R	153.1	
	13.8	Ribble Trail, north junction	w	153.0	
	19.3	Wapiti Shelter (2,600')	Sw	147.5	
	21.1	Stream	w	145.7	
	21.4	Ribble Trail, south junction		145.4	
	23.5	Walnut Flats Campground (C,w 0.4m W)	Cw	143.3	
	25.4	Dismal Creek Falls Trail		141.4	
	27.3	Va. 606 (2,040') (C,G,M,w 0.5m W)	RCGMw	139.5	
	27.4	Kimberling Creek		139.4	
	29.2	Brushy Mountain (2,800')		137.6	
	32.6	Va. 608, Lickskillet Hollow (2,200')	R	134.2	
	33.8	Jenny Knob Shelter	Sw	133.0	
	35.5	Brushy Mountain (3,101')		131.3	
	36.9	Va. 611	R	129.9	
	43.5	Helveys Mill Shelter (S,w 0.3m E)	Sw	123.3	
	44.9	Va. 612, Kimberling Creek	R	121.9	
	45.3	I-77 Crossing	R	121.5	

Roanoke A.T. Club — Va. Section 34 — Va. 35 — OCVT — Va. Section 36

SW Va. Map 1 — Map 2

Southwest Virginia

Miles from New River, Va.   *Miles from Damascus, Va.*

GBS	N to S	Features	Facilities	S to N	Map
	45.7	U.S. 52 (2,920'); **Bastian, Va., P.O. 24314; Bland, Va., P.O. 24315** ☆			
		(P.O. 1.8m W; P.O.,G,L,M 2.7m E)	RGLM	121.1	
Va. Section 37	52.6	Va. 615, Laurel Creek (2,450')	RCw	114.2	
	53.4	Brushy Mountain (3,080')		113.4	
	57.0	Jenkins Shelter (2,470')	Sw	109.8	
	57.9	Stream	w	108.9	
	60.5	Davis Farm Campsite (C,w 0.4m W)	Cw	106.3	
	61.5	Va. 623, Garden Mountain (3,880')	R	105.3	
	66.3	Walker Gap (3,520') (w 0.2m E)	Rw	100.5	SW Va. Map 2
Va. Section 38	67.7	Chestnut Knob Shelter (4,409')	S(nw)	99.1	
	69.5	Spring-fed pond	w	97.3	Piedmont A.T. Hikers
	72.3	USFS 222 (2,300')	R	94.5	
	73.7	Lick Creek	w	93.1	
	76.0	Lynn Camp Creek (2,400')	w	90.8	
	76.6	Campsite, stream	Cw	90.2	
	77.1	Knot Maul Branch Shelter	S	89.7	
	78.3	Brushy Mountain (3,200')		88.5	
	79.2	Va. 42; **Ceres, Va., P.O. 24318**	R	87.6	
	79.8	Spring	w	87.0	
	80.2	Va. 742, North Fork of Holston River		86.6	
Va. Section 39	81.7	Va. 610	R	85.1	
	83.2	Tilson Gap, Big Walker Mountain (3,500')		83.6	
	85.1	Crawfish Valley (2,600')	Cw	81.7	Map 3
	86.2	Little Brushy Mountain (3,300')		80.6	
	89.0	Davis Path Campsite	C(nw)	77.8	
	90.1	Spring	w	76.7	
	90.8	Va. 617	R	76.0	

Southwest Virginia

		Miles from New River, Va.		*Miles from Damascus, Va.*	
	91.8	Va. 683, U.S. 11, I-81 (2,420'); **Atkins, Va., P.O. 24311** (P.O. 3.1m W; G,L,M on A.T.)	RGLM	75.0	
	94.1	Va. 729	R	72.7	
	94.6	Va. 615	R	72.2	
	96.1	USFS 644	R	70.7	
	96.4	Chatfield Shelter	Sw	70.4	
	97.9	Glade Mountain (4,093')		68.9	
	99.2	USFS 86	Cw	67.6	
	99.6	Locust Mountain		67.2	
	100.6	Brushy Mountain		66.2	
	102.5	Va. 622	R	64.3	
	103.2	Va. 16 (3,220'); **Sugar Grove, Va., P.O. 24375** **Marion, Va., P.O. 24354** (P.O.,G 3.1m E; P.O., G,L,M 6.6m W)	☆ RGLMw	63.6	
	103.4	Partnership Shelter	Sw	63.4	
	107.3	Va. 601	R	59.5	
	111.1	Va. 670 (Teas Road), South Fork Holston River (2,450')	R	55.7	
	112.0	Va. 672	R	54.8	
	113.2	Trimpi Shelter	Sw	53.6	
	115.3	High Point (4,040')		51.5	
	115.8	Bobby's Trail, Raccoon Branch Campground (C,w 0.2m E; 3.3m E)	Cw	51.0	
	117.3	Dickey Gap, Va. 16, Va. 650; **Troutdale, Va., P.O. 24378** (P.O. 2.7m E; L 2.3m E)	RL	49.5	
	118.5	Comers Creek, Comers Creek Falls Trail (3,200')	w	48.3	

Left margin labels (top to bottom): Va. Section 40 · Mt. Rogers A.T. Club · Piedmont A.T. Hikers · Va. Section 41 · Va. Sec. 42

Right margin label: SW Va. Map 3

Southwest Virginia

GBS	N to S	Features	Facilities (see page 8 for codes)		S to N	Map
		Miles from New River, Va.			*Miles from Damascus, Va.*	
	119.3	Dickey Gap Trail				
		(C,w 0.4m W)		Cw	47.5	
	121.0	Stream		w	45.8	
	121.8	Hurricane Creek Trail			45.0	
	122.4	Hurricane Mountain Shelter		Sw	44.4	
	123.3	Chestnut Flats, Iron Mountain Trail			43.5	
	123.6	Hurricane Mountain (4,320'),				
		Tennessee-New River Divide			43.2	
	125.6	Va. 603, Fox Creek (3,480')				
		(C,w on A.T., 1.9m W)		RCw	41.2	
	127.3	Old Orchard Shelter		Sw	39.5	
	128.9	Pine Mountain Trail (5,000')			37.9	
	130.3	The Scales			36.5	
	130.7	Stone Mountain			36.1	
	133.0	Wilson Creek Trail				
		(Cw 1.3m E)		Cw	33.8	
	133.2	Big Wilson Creek		Cw	33.6	
	133.3	Grayson Highlands State Park,				
		Wise Shelter (4,460')		Sw	33.5	
	135.4	Park service road to Massie Gap			31.4	
	136.2	Wilburn Ridge			30.6	
	137.4	Rhododendron Gap (5,440')			29.4	
	138.4	Thomas Knob Shelter		Sw	28.4	
	138.6	Mt. Rogers Spur Trail			28.2	
	140.6	Deep Gap (w 0.2m E)		w	26.2	
	142.6	Va. 600, Elk Garden (4,434')		R	24.2	
	145.0	Whitetop Mountain Road (USFS 89)		R	21.8	
	145.1	Spring		w	21.7	
	145.9	Buzzard Rock (5,080'),				
		Whitetop Mountain			20.9	

Left margin: Va. Section 42 · Va. Section 43 · Sec. 44

Right margin: SW Va. Map 3 · Mt. Rogers A.T. Club · SW Va. Map 4

Southwest Virginia

GBS	N to S	Features	Facilities (see page 8 for codes)	S to N	Map
	Miles from New River, Va.		*Miles from Damascus, Va.*		
	148.4	Va. 601 (Beech Mountain Road)	Rw	18.4	
	149.7	U.S. 58 (3,160'); Summit Cut, Va.	R	17.1	
	150.8	Lost Mountain Shelter	Sw	16.0	
	152.0	Va. 859 (Grassy Ridge Road)	R	14.8	
	152.6	Virginia Creeper Trail, Whitetop Laurel Creek		14.2	
	153.2	Va. 728, Creek Junction (2,720') (R 0.5m E)	R	13.6	
	154.8	Campsite	Cw	12.0	
	155.0	Bear Tree Gap side trail (C 0.6m W)	C	11.8	
	157.3	Saunders Shelter (S,w 0.2m W)	Sw	9.5	
	157.6	Straight Mountain (3,500')		9.2	
	159.2	Taylors Valley Side Trail (M 0.6m E)	M	7.6	
	159.8	Stream	w	7.0	
	161.2	U.S. 58, Straight Branch, Feathercamp Branch (2,200'), Feathercamp Trail	Rw	5.6	
	161.8	Beech Grove Trail		5.0	
	163.3	Feathercamp Ridge, Iron Mountain Trail (2,850')		3.5	
	165.8	U.S. 58, Va. 91, Virginia Creeper Trail	R	1.0	
	166.8	**Damascus, Va., P.O. 24236** (1,928') (P.O.,G,L,M on A.T.)	☆ RGLM	0.0	

Mt. Rogers A.T. Club
Va. Section 45

SW Va. Map 4

GBS	N to S	Features	Facilities (see page 8 for codes)	S to N	Map

Miles from Damascus, Va.

Miles from Fontana Dam, N.C.

	N to S	Features	Facilities	S to N
	0.0	**Damascus, Va., P.O. 24236** (1,928')	☆	
		(P.O.,G,L,M on A.T.)	RGLM	302.6
	2.1	Spring	w	300.5
	3.7	Virginia–Tennessee Line		298.9
	10.2	Abingdon Gap Shelter (3,785')	CSw	292.4
	11.3	McQueens Gap, USFS 69	R	291.3
	11.7	McQueens Knob		290.9
	13.1	Double Spring Gap	w	289.5
	15.0	Low Gap, U.S. 421 (3,384');		
		Shady Valley, Tenn., P.O. 37688		
		(w on A.T.; P.O.,G,M 3m E)	RGMw	287.6
	18.5	Double Springs Shelter,		
		Holston Mountain Trail (4,080')	Sw	284.1
	19.4	Campsite	w	283.2
	21.5	Tenn. 91 (3,450')	R	281.1
	22.3	Stream	w	280.3
	24.7	Spring	w	277.9
	24.8	Nick Grindstaff Monument		277.8
	26.1	Iron Mountain Shelter (4,125')	S(nw)	276.5
	26.3	Spring	w	276.3
	27.7	Turkeypen Gap		274.9
	29.1	Spring	w	273.5
	32.9	Vandeventer Shelter (3,510')		
		(S on A.T.; w 0.5m W)	Sw	269.7
	34.6	Spring	w	268.0
	37.6	Wilbur Dam Road	R	265.0
	38.9	Watauga Dam (north end)		263.7
	40.1	Watauga Lake Shelter (2,100')	Sw	262.5
	40.5	Griffith Branch	w	262.1

Left margin (top to bottom): Tenn.–N.C. Section 1 · Tenn.–N.C. Section 2 · Tenn.–N.C. Section 3 · Tenn.–N.C. Sec. 4

Right margin: MRATC · Tennessee Eastman Hiking Club · Tenn.–N.C. Map 1

Tennessee–North Carolina

GBS	N to S	Features	Facilities (see page 8 for codes)	S to N	Map
	Miles from Damascus, Va.			*Miles from Fontana Dam, N.C.*	
	42.0	U.S. 321; **Hampton, Tenn., P.O. 37658** (P.O.,G,M 2.6m W; G,L 1.8m W)	RGLM	260.6	
	42.5	Campsite	C	260.1	
	45.1	Pond Flats	Cw	257.5	
	47.9	Side trail to U.S. 321	w	254.7	
	48.4	Waycaster Spring	w	254.2	
	48.7	Laurel Fork Shelter (2,400')	Sw	253.9	
	49.4	Laurel Fork Falls	w	253.2	
	50.6	Dennis Cove, USFS 50 (C,G,L,M 0.5m E; C,L 0.2m W)	RCGLMw	252.0	
	52.3	Trail to Coon Den Falls		250.3	
	54.8	Campsite	Cw	247.8	
	55.7	White Rocks Mountain (4,206')		246.9	
	56.9	Moreland Gap Shelter	Sw	245.7	
	60.0	Campsite, stream	Cw	242.6	
	62.7	Laurel Fork		239.9	
	63.7	Stream		238.9	
	64.9	Walnut Mountain Road	R	237.7	
	65.7	Campsite	Cw	236.9	
	66.5	Mountaineer Falls Shelter	Sw	236.1	
	66.7	Campsite	Cw	235.9	
	68.9	Campsite	Cw	233.7	
	71.7	Campbell Hollow Road	R	230.9	
	72.0	Buck Mountain Road	R	230.6	
	75.1	Bear Branch Road	R	227.5	

Side labels: *Tennessee Eastman Hiking Club*; Tenn.–N.C. 4; Tenn.–N.C. Section 5; Tenn.–N.C. Map 1; Tenn.–N.C. Map 2

Tennessee–North Carolina

GBS	N to S	Features	Facilities (see page 8 for codes)	S to N	Map
	Miles from Damascus, Va.		*Miles from Fontana Dam, N.C.*		
Tenn.–N.C. Section 6	75.3	U.S. 19E (2,895'); **Roan Mountain, Tenn., P.O. 37687; Elk Park, N.C., P.O. 28622** (P.O.,G,M 3.4m W; P.O. 2.5m E; C 4.0m E; G 1.2m E; L 3m E; M 0.5m E, 1m E)	☆ RCGLM	227.3	Tenn.–N.C. Map 2 · Tennessee Eastman Hiking Club
	75.9	Campsite	Cw	226.7	
	78.3	Doll Flats	Cw	224.3	
	80.7	Hump Mountain (5,587')		221.9	
	81.6	Bradley Gap	Cw	221.0	
	82.9	Little Hump Mountain (5,459')	Cw	219.7	
	84.5	Yellow Mountain Gap, Overmountain Shelter (4,682') (w 0.2m E; C,S 0.3m E)	CSw	218.1	
	86.4	Stan Murray Shelter (5,050')	Sw	216.2	
Tenn.–N.C. 7	88.2	Side trail to Grassy Ridge		214.4	
	90.1	Carvers Gap, Tenn. 143, N.C. 261 (5,512')	Rw	212.5	
	91.6	Roan High Knob Shelter (6,285')	Sw	211.0	
	93.7	Ash Gap	Cw	208.9	
Tenn.–N.C. Section 8	96.7	Hughes Gap (4,040') (G 3.2m W; C,L 2m E)	RCGL	205.9	
	98.9	Little Rock Knob (4,918')		203.7	
	100.1	Clyde Smith Shelter	Sw	202.5	
	101.2	Campsite	Cw	201.4	
	102.0	Greasy Creek Gap (4,034') (C,w 0.2m W; L 0.7m E)	CLw	200.6	
	104.9	Campsite	Cw	197.7	
Sec. 9	106.1	Iron Mountain Gap, Tenn. 107, N.C. 226 (3,723') (G 4.7m W)	RG	196.5	

Tennessee–North Carolina

GBS	N to S	Features	Facilities (see page 8 for codes)	S to N	Map

Miles from Damascus, Va.

Miles from Fontana Dam, N.C.

		Features	Facilities		
	109.2	Cherry Gap Shelter	Sw	193.4	
	110.3	Low Gap (3,900')	w	192.3	
	112.5	Unaka Mountain (5,180')		190.1	
	113.5	USFS 230	R	189.1	
	114.1	Deep Gap (4,100')	Cw	188.5	
	115.1	Beauty Spot Gap	Rw	187.5	
	115.6	Beauty Spot		187.0	
	116.8	USFS 230	R	185.8	
	117.9	Indian Grave Gap, Tenn. 395 C 3.3m W)	RC	184.7	
	122.0	Curley Maple Gap Shelter (3,070')	Sw	180.6	
	124.9	Nolichucky River Valley (C,L,M on A.T.)	RCLM	177.7	
	126.2	Nolichucky River (1,700'); **Erwin, Tenn., P.O. 37650** (P.O.,G,M 3.8m W; L 1.2m W; G,L 2.3m W)	RGLM	176.4	
	130.1	Temple Hill Gap (2,850')		172.5	
	132.5	No Business Knob Shelter	CS	170.1	
	132.7	Spring	w	169.9	
	136.8	Oglesby Branch	w	165.8	
	137.4	Spivey Gap, U.S. 19W (3,200')	Rw	165.2	
	137.9	Campsite	Cw	164.7	
	139.4	Trail to High Rocks (4,100')		163.2	
	139.7	Whistling Gap	Cw	162.9	
	141.7	Little Bald		160.9	
	142.7	Campsite	Cw	159.9	
	143.1	Bald Mountain Shelter	Sw	159.5	
	144.0	Big Stamp (C,w 0.3m W; M 1.5m E)	CMw	158.6	

Left margin labels: Tenn.–N.C. Section 9 · Tennessee Eastman Hiking Club · Tenn.–N.C. Section 10 · Carolina Mountain Club · Tenn.–N.C. Section 11

Right margin labels: Tenn.–N.C. Map 2 · Tenn.–N.C. Map 3

Tennessee–North Carolina

GBS	N to S	Features	Facilities (see page 8 for codes)	S to N	Map
	Miles from Damascus, Va.			*Miles from Fontana Dam, N.C.*	
	144.3	Big Bald (5,516')		158.3	
	145.1	Spring	w	157.5	
	147.1	Low Gap	w	155.5	
	148.5	Street Gap (4,100')		154.1	
	150.1	Springs	w	152.5	
	150.8	Sams Gap, U.S. 23, I-26 (3,800') (M 1.9m E, 2.8m E; G 3.2m E)	RGM	151.8	
	152.6	High Rock (4,460')		150.0	
	153.2	Hogback Ridge Shelter (C,S 0.1m E; w 0.3m E)	CSw	149.4	
	154.4	Rice Gap (3,800')		148.2	
	155.4	Big Flat	C	147.2	
	156.0	Frozen Knob (4,579')		146.6	
	158.8	Rector Laurel Road (2,960')	R	143.8	
	159.3	Devil Fork Gap, N.C. 212	R	143.3	
	161.1	Campsite	Cw	141.5	
	162.0	Flint Mountain Shelter (3,550')	Sw	140.6	
	163.6	Spring	w	139.0	
	166.8	Big Butt (4,750')	C	135.8	
	168.7	Jerry Cabin Shelter (4,150')	Sw	133.9	
	171.2	Big Firescald Knob	w	131.4	
	172.2	Blackstack Cliffs (0.1m W)		130.4	
	172.4	White Rock Cliffs (0.1m E		130.2	
	172.5	Spring	w	130.1	
	174.2	Camp Creek Bald, side trail to fire tower (4,750')	R	128.4	
	176.0	Little Laurel Shelter (3,300')	CSw	126.6	
	180.9	Allen Gap, N.C. 208, Tenn. 70 (2,234')	Rw	121.7	
	183.1	Spring	w	119.5	
	184.6	Spring Mountain Shelter (3,300')	CSw	118.0	

Tenn.–N.C. 11 — Tenn.–N.C. Section 12 — Tenn.–N.C. Section 13

Tenn.–N.C. Map 3 — Carolina Mountain Club

Tennessee–North Carolina

GBS	N to S	Features	Facilities (see page 8 for codes)	S to N	Map
		Miles from Damascus, Va.	*Miles from* Fontana Dam, N.C.		
	186.3	Hurricane Gap	R	116.3	
	187.4	Rich Mountain Fire Tower			
		Side Trail (3,600')	Cw	115.2	
	189.7	Tanyard Gap, U.S. 25 & 70 (2,278')	R	112.9	
	190.7	Campsite	C	111.9	
	192.3	Pump Gap		110.3	
	194.2	Lovers Leap Rock		108.4	
	195.6	U.S. 25 & 70, N.C. 209 (1,326');			
		Hot Springs, N.C., P.O. 28743	☆		
		(P.O.,C,G,L,M on A.T.)	RCGLM	107.0	
	198.8	Deer Park Mountain Shelter	CSw	103.8	
	202.2	Garenflo Gap (2,500')	R	100.4	
	204.7	Big Rock Spring	w	97.9	
	206.3	Bluff Mountain (4,686')		96.3	
	208.7	Walnut Mountain Shelter (C 0.1m W)	CSw	93.9	
	210.0	Lemon Gap, N.C. 1182,			
		Tenn. 107 (3,550')	R	92.6	
	213.5	Roaring Fork Shelter	CSw	89.1	
	215.4	Max Patch Summit (4,629')		87.2	
	216.2	Max Patch Road (N.C. 1182)	R	86.4	
	218.9	Brown Gap	Rw	83.7	
	221.8	Deep Gap, Groundhog Creek Shelter (2,900')			
		(C,S,w 0.2m E)	CSw	80.8	
	223.8	Campsite	Cw	78.8	
	224.3	Snowbird Mountain (4,263')	R	78.3	
	225.8	Spanish Oak Gap		76.8	
	226.7	Painter Branch	Cw	75.9	
	229.0	Green Corner Road			
		(C,G,L 0.2m W)	RCGL	73.6	
	229.5	I-40	R	73.1	

Left margin labels: Tenn.–N.C. Sec. 14 · Tenn.–N.C. Section 15 · Tenn.–N.C. Section 16 · Carolina Mountain Club

Right margin label: Tenn.–N.C. Map 4

Tennessee–North Carolina

Tenn.–N.C. Map 4
CMC
Smoky Mountains Hiking Club
Great Smoky Mtns. N.P. Map
Tenn.–N.C. Section 17 (N.C. 1)

GBS	N to S	Features	Facilities (see page 8 for codes)	S to N	Map
	Miles from Damascus, Va.			*Miles from Fontana Dam, N.C.*	
	229.9	Pigeon River (1,400')		72.7	
	230.1	State Line Branch	Cw	72.5	
	231.4	Davenport Gap, Tenn. 32, S.R. 1397; eastern boundary, Great Smoky Mountains National Park (1,975') (C 2.5m E)	RC	71.2	
	232.3	Davenport Gap Shelter	Sw	70.3	
	234.5	Spring	w	68.1	
	236.0	Spring	w	66.6	
	236.5	Mt. Cammerer Side Trail (5,000')		66.1	
	238.6	Low Gap Trail		64.0	
	239.4	Cosby Knob Shelter	Sw	63.2	
	239.8	Cosby Knob		62.8	
	243.1	Snake Den Ridge Trail		59.5	
	245.1	Guyot Spring	w	57.5	
	245.7	Guyot Spur (6,360')		56.9	
	247.1	Tri-Corner Knob Shelter	Sw	55.5	
	247.9	Mt. Chapman		54.7	
	249.6	Mt. Sequoyah		53.0	
	251.9	Pecks Corner Shelter (w on A.T.; S,w 0.5m E)	Sw	50.7	
	253.9	Bradleys View		48.7	
	257.0	Porters Gap, The Sawteeth		45.6	
	258.3	Charlies Bunion		44.3	
	259.2	Icewater Spring Shelter	Sw	43.4	
	259.5	Boulevard Trail to Mt. LeConte		43.1	
	262.2	Newfound Gap, U.S. 441 (5,045')	Rw	40.4	
	263.9	Indian Gap	R	38.7	
	266.5	Mt. Collins Shelter (5,900') (S,w 0.5m W)	Sw	36.1	

Tennessee–North Carolina

GBS	N to S	Features	Facilities (see page 8 for codes)	S to N	Map
	Miles from Damascus, Va.		*Miles from Fontana Dam, N.C.*		
	269.1	Mt. Love		33.5	
	269.9	Clingmans Dome (6,643') (R,w 0.5m E)	Rw	32.7	
	272.6	Double Spring Gap Shelter (5,507')	Sw	30.0	
	274.1	Silers Bald		28.5	
	274.3	Silers Bald Shelter	Sw	28.3	
	277.3	Buckeye Gap (4,817')	w	25.3	
	279.8	Sams Gap	w	22.8	
	280.0	Derrick Knob Shelter	Sw	22.6	
	281.0	Sugar Tree Gap (4,435')		21.6	
	282.7	Mineral Gap (5,030')		19.9	
	283.3	Beechnut Gap	w	19.3	
	284.3	Thunderhead, east peak (5,527')		18.3	
	284.9	Rocky Top		17.7	
	286.1	Eagle Creek Trail to Spence Field Shelter, Bote Mountain Trail (S,w 0.2m E)	Sw	16.5	
	288.9	Russell Field Shelter	Sw	13.7	
	290.3	Little Abrams Gap (4,120')		12.3	
	291.3	Devils Tater Patch (4,775')		11.3	
	292.0	Mollies Ridge Shelter	Sw	10.6	
	293.7	Ekaneetlee Gap (3,842')	w	8.9	
	295.1	Doe Knob (4,520')		7.5	
	297.2	Birch Spring Gap	Cw	5.4	
	298.5	Shuckstack fire tower (0.1m E)		4.1	
	302.6	Little Tennessee River, Fontana Dam; southern boundary, Great Smoky Mountains National Park (1,800')	R	0.0	

Smoky Mountains Hiking Club

Tenn.–N.C. Section 18 (N.C. 2)

Great Smoky Mtns. N.P. Map

GBS	N to S	Features	Facilities (see page 8 for codes)	S to N	Map

Miles from Fontana Dam, N.C.

Miles from Springer Mountain, Ga.

	N to S	Features	Facilities	S to N	
	0.0	Little Tennessee River, Fontana Dam; southern boundary, Great Smoky Mountains National Park (1,740')	R	166.4	
	0.4	Fontana Dam Visitor Center	Rw	166.0	
N.C. Section 3	0.8	Fontana Dam Shelter	CSw	165.6	
	2.0	N.C. 28;			
		Fontana Dam, N.C., P.O. 28733	☆		
		(P.O.,G,L,M 1.8m W)	RGLM	164.4	
	4.3	Campsite	Cw	162.1	
	4.7	Walker Gap (3,450')		161.7	
	6.1	Black Gum Gap		160.3	
	7.5	Cable Gap Shelter	CSw	158.9	
N.C. Section 4	8.4	Yellow Creek Gap, S.R. 1242 (2,980') (Yellow Creek Mountain Road) (L 4m E)	RL	158.0	N.C.–Ga. Map 1
	10.8	Cody Gap	Cw	155.6	
	11.6	Hogback Gap		154.8	
	13.4	Brown Fork Gap	w	153.0	
	13.6	Brown Fork Gap Shelter	Sw	152.8	*Smoky Mountains Hiking Club*
	15.0	Sweetwater Gap		151.4	
	16.0	Stecoah Gap, N.C. 143 (3,165') (Sweetwater Creek Road)	Rw	150.4	
N.C. Section 5	18.1	Simp Gap		148.3	
	19.1	Locust Cove Gap	Cw	147.3	
	21.5	Cheoah Bald (5,062')		144.9	
	22.7	Sassafras Gap Shelter	CSw	143.7	
	23.6	Swim Bald		142.8	
	26.5	Grassy Gap (3,050')		139.9	
	28.0	Wright Gap	R	138.4	

North Carolina–Georgia

Miles from
Fontana Dam, N.C.

Miles from
Springer Mountain, Ga.

	N to S	Features	Facilities	S to N
	29.6	U.S. 19, U.S. 74, Nantahala River (1,723'); Wesser, N.C. (L,M on A.T.; G 1m E)	RGLM	136.8
	30.4	A. Rufus Morgan Shelter	CSw	136.0
	33.5	Jump-up Lookout (4,000')		132.9
	35.3	Wesser Creek Trail, Wesser Bald Shelter	CS	131.1
	35.4	Spring	w	131.0
	36.1	Wesser Bald (4,627'), viewing tower (0.1m E)		130.3
	37.5	Tellico Gap, S.R. 1365 (3,850')	R	128.9
	38.9	Spring	w	127.5
	39.2	Side trail to Rocky Bald Lookout		127.2
	40.4	Copper Ridge Bald Lookout (5,080')		126.0
	41.1	Cold Spring Shelter	CSw	125.3
	42.3	Burningtown Gap, S.R. 1397 (4,236')	R	124.1
	44.6	Licklog Gap (C 0.1 W, w 0.5m W)	Cw	121.8
	45.9	Wayah Shelter	CSw	120.5
	46.4	Campsite	Cw	120.0
	46.8	Wayah Bald (5,342')	R	119.6
	48.7	Wine Spring	Cw	117.7
	49.2	USFS 69	Rw	117.2
	51.0	Wayah Gap, S.R. 1310 (4,180')	R	115.4
	52.7	Siler Bald Shelter (4,700') (C,S,w 0.5m E)	CSw	113.7
	54.9	Panther Gap		111.5
	55.8	Swinging Lick Gap		110.6
	56.0	Campsite	Cw	110.4

Nantahala Hiking Club

N.C. Section 6
N.C. Section 7
N.C. Section 8

N.C.–Ga. Map 2

North Carolina–Georgia

Miles from Fontana Dam, N.C. *Miles from Springer Mountain, Ga.*

	N to S	Features	Facilities	S to N	
N.C. 8	56.9	Winding Stair Gap, U.S. 64;			N.C.–Ga. Map 2
		Franklin, N.C., P.O. 28734	☆		
		(w on A.T.; P.O.,G,L,M 10m E)	RGLMw	109.5	
	60.0	Wallace Gap, "Old 64" (3,738')	R	106.4	
	60.6	Rock Gap, Standing Indian Campground			
		(C 1.5m W)	RC	105.8	
	60.7	Rock Gap Shelter	Sw	105.7	
	63.2	Glassmine Gap		103.2	
	64.1	Long Branch Shelter	CSw	102.3	
	66.6	Albert Mountain (5,250')		99.8	
N.C. Section 9	66.9	Bearpen Trail, USFS 67	R	99.5	
	67.9	Spring	w	98.5	
	68.2	Mooney Gap, USFS 83	R	98.2	
	69.1	Betty Creek Gap (4,300')	Cw	97.3	
	72.8	Carter Gap Shelter	CSw	93.6	
	73.2	Timber Ridge Trail		93.2	
	76.0	Beech Gap (4,460')	Cw	90.4	
	78.9	Lower Trail Ridge Trail,			
		Standing Indian Mountain (5,498')			
		(w 0.2m W)	w	87.5	
	80.4	Standing Indian Shelter	CSw	86.0	
N.C. Section 10	81.3	Deep Gap, USFS 71 (4,341') (C 0.1m W)	CRw	85.1	Nantahala Hiking Club
	83.4	Wateroak Gap		83.0	
	84.3	Chunky Gal Trail		82.1	
	84.5	Whiteoak Stamp	w	81.9	
	85.3	Muskrat Creek Shelter (4,600')	CSw	81.1	
	86.2	Sassafras Gap		80.2	
	88.1	Bly Gap (3,840')	Cw	78.3	
	88.2	North Carolina–Georgia Line		78.2	GATC
	90.1	Rich Cove Gap		76.3	

North Carolina–Georgia

Miles from Fontana Dam, N.C.

Miles from Springer Mountain, Ga.

	N to S	Features	Facilities	S to N
Ga. Section 11	90.3	Campsite	Cw	76.1
	91.3	Blue Ridge Gap (3,020')		75.1
	91.9	As Knob		74.5
	92.6	Plumorchard Gap Shelter (C,S,w 0.2m E)	CSw	73.8
	93.8	Bull Gap (3,550')		72.6
	95.3	Cowart Gap		71.1
	96.0	Campsite	Cw	70.4
	97.1	Dicks Creek Gap, U.S. 76 (2,675'); **Hiawassee, Ga., P.O. 30546** (w on A.T.; L 3.5m W; P.O.,G,L,M 11m W)	☆ RGLMw	69.3
Ga. Section 12	97.7	Streams	w	68.7
	98.3	Moreland Gap		68.1
	99.3	Powell Mountain (3,850')		67.1
	99.5	McClure Gap	C	66.9
	100.7	Deep Gap Shelter (3,550') (C,S,w 0.3m E)	CSw	65.7
	101.5	Kelly Knob (4,276')		64.9
	102.5	Addis Gap (3,304') (C,w 0.5m E)	Cw	63.9
	103.4	Sassafras Gap	w	63.0
	104.5	Swag of the Blue Ridge		61.9
	108.1	Tray Mountain Shelter (C,S 0.2m W; w 0.3m W)	CSw	58.3
	108.6	Tray Mountain (4,430')		57.8
	109.4	Tray Gap, Tray Mountain Road (USFS 79/698)	R	57.0
	110.1	Cheese Factory Site	Cw	56.3
	110.4	Tray Mountain Road (USFS 79)	R	56.0

Georgia A.T. Club

N.C.–Ga. Map 3

A.T. Maintaining Clubs

Maine A.T. Club	www.matc.org
Appalachian Mountain Club	www.outdoors.org
Randolph Mountain Club	www.randolphmountainclub.org
Dartmouth Outing Club	outdoors.dartmouth.edu
Green Mountain Club	www.greenmountainclub.org
AMC Berkshire Chapter	www.amcberkshire.org
AMC Connecticut Chapter	www.ct-amc.org
New York–New Jersey Trail Conference	www.nynjtc.org
Wilmington Trail Club	www.wilmingtontrailclub.org
Batona Hiking Club	www.batonawildapricot.org
AMC Delaware Valley Chapter	www.amcdv.org
Keystone Trails Association	www.kta-hike.org
Blue Mountain Eagle Climbing Club	www.bmecc.org
Allentown Hiking Club	www.allentownhikingclub.org
Susquehanna A.T. Club	www.satc-hike.org
York Hiking Club	www.yorkhikingclub.com
Cumberland Valley A.T. Club	www.cvatclub.org
Mountain Club of Maryland	www.mcomd.org
Potomac A.T. Club	www.patc.net
Old Dominion A.T. Club	www.odatc.net
Tidewater A.T. Club	www.tidewateratc.org
Natural Bridge A.T. Club	www.nbatc.org
Roanoke A.T. Club	www.ratc.org
Outdoor Club of Virginia Tech	www.outdoor.org.vt.edu
Piedmont A.T. Hikers	www.path-at.org
Mount Rogers A.T. Club	www.mratc.org
Tennessee Eastman Hiking Club	www.tehcc.org
Carolina Mountain Club	www.carolinamountainclub.org
Smoky Mountains Hiking Club	www.smhclub.org
Nantahala Hiking Club	www.nantahalahikingclub.org
Georgia A.T. Club	www.georgia-atclub.org

History of the *Appalachian Trail Data Book*

The model for the *Appalachian Trail Data Book* was the "Mileage Fact Sheet" compiled by Ed Garvey and Gus Crews, published simultaneously in 1971 by the Appalachian Trail Conference and Appalachian Books (Oakton, Va.) as an appendix to Mr. Garvey's *Appalachian Hiker*.

The first edition (1977) of the *Appalachian Trail Data Book* was compiled by Raymond F. Hunt of Kingsport, Tenn., who continued to perform this volunteer service annually until 1983, when he began a six-year term as chair of the ATC.

The editions since then have been compiled by another volunteer, Daniel D. Chazin of Teaneck, N.J., an officer of the New York–New Jersey Trail Conference and editor of the *Appalachian Trail Guide to New York–New Jersey.* Mr. Chazin draws each fall on the work of editors of the other 10 guidebooks, more than 30 other volunteer data compilers, and Conservancy regional offices for information on the various sections of the Appalachian Trail.

The Appalachian Trail Community Network

The Appalachian Trail Community program is an ATC initiative that seeks to develop mutually beneficial relationships with interested towns and counties along the Trail—to enhance their economies, further protect the Trail, and engage a new generation of volunteers.

Communities designated as of December 2016 were:

Millinocket, Maine
Monson, Maine
Kingfield, Maine
Rangeley, Maine
Hanover, New Hampshire
Norwich, Vermont
North Adams, Massachusetts
Great Barrington, Massachusetts
Harlem Valley (Dover and Pawling),
    New York
Warwick, New York
Delaware Water Gap, Pennsylvania
Wind Gap, Pennsylvania
Duncannon, Pennsylvania
Boiling Springs, Pennsylvania
Greater Waynesboro, Pennsylvania
Harpers Ferry/Bolivar, West Virginia
Berryville/Clarke County, Virginia
Front Royal/Warren County, Virginia
Luray/Page County, Virginia
Harrisonburg, Virginia
Nelson County, Virginia
Waynesboro, Virginia
Buena Vista, Virginia
Glasgow, Virginia
Troutville, Virginia
Narrows, Virginia
Pearisburg, Virginia
Bland, Virginia

Marion/Smyth County, Virginia
Abingdon, Virginia
Damascus, Virginia
Roan Mountain, Tennessee
Erwin/Unicoi County, Tennessee
Hot Springs, North Carolina
Fontana Dam, North Carolina
Franklin, North Carolina
Hiawassee/Towns County, Georgia
Helen/White County, Georgia
Union County (Blairsville, Suches),
    Georgia
Dahlonega, Georgia
Ellijay/Gilmer County, Georgia

Those listed in the *Data Book* are indicated by a ☆ in the Facilities column.

Protect, enhance, and promote

the Trail experience:

That's what we do.

You can help
by joining the
Appalachian Trail Conservancy
today!

You can become a member
by going to
www.appalachiantrail.org/join
or calling
(304) 535-6331